THE *INDIANAPOLIS* *500*

RED ⚡ LIGHTNING BOOKS

THE *INDIANAPOLIS*
500 INSIDE THE GREATEST SPECTACLE IN RACING

James Craig Reinhardt

This book is a publication of

Red Lightning Books
1320 East 10th Street
Bloomington, Indiana 47405 USA

redlightningbooks.com

© 2019 by Indiana University Press

All photographs in this publication have been sourced through the
Indianapolis Motor Speedway Photo Shop and used with permission
of the Indianapolis Motor Speedway except for the following:

Winner's Ring courtesy of Ken Keltner for Herff-Jones.

Proceeds from the sale of this book benefit the activities of the
Indianapolis Motor Speedway Museum Foundation and its mission
to celebrate more than a century of the innovation, thrill, and
adventure of motor racing at the Indianapolis Motor Speedway.

Thank you for your support.

Manufactured in the United States of America

ISBN: 978-1-68435-074-2 (paperback)
ISBN: 978-1-68435-076-6 (ebook)

1 2 3 4 5 24 23 22 21 20 19

For

BILL, JAMES, KELLIE, KERRIE,
KRISTA, AND KATHRYN

Contents

PART 2 🏎️ THE MONTH OF MAY

PART 3 🏎 RACE DAY

PART 4 🏎 EPILOGUE

Preface

As a tour guide at the Indianapolis Motor Speedway, I have the opportunity to share in the history and many of the traditions of the World's Greatest Race Course and the Indianapolis 500-Mile Race with thousands of guests. Why winners drink milk, why it's called the Brickyard, and why winners kiss the bricks are three of the better-known topics addressed during a tour, but time does not permit the presentation of the fascinating stories and history behind dozens of other customs that have been celebrated for decades. This book is an attempt to share those stories with the veteran race fan and rookie fan alike.

I hope you will enjoy and embrace the Greatest Spectacle in Racing!

JAMES CRAIG REINHARDT
The Cottage at Turn One
Speedway, Indiana
October 2018

Acknowledgments

Compiling, writing, and editing a publication highlighting and describing the better-known traditions of the Indianapolis Motor Speedway and the Indianapolis 500-Mile Race required the help and support of literally dozens of people. Each of those listed below has his or her area of expertise, and I relied on each and every one to produce a book I hope will be interesting and informative for all fans.

Donald Davidson is the historian at the Indianapolis Motor Speedway. No one knows more about the facility or the 500 than he. Much of the material in this book is that which he has researched and compiled over the past several decades. I simply tried to organize the information in a logical and cohesive format. He took his own time to proofread and review the initial manuscript for content and accuracy. I could not be more grateful.

Betsy Smith is executive director of the Indianapolis Motor Speedway Foundation. She believed in the project and me from the very beginning. She was instrumental in securing contacts and a publisher. Most importantly, she was a constant source of encouragement.

The staff at the Indianapolis Motor Speedway Museum includes tour bus drivers, museum hosts and hostesses, office personnel, and tour guides. These individuals are my coworkers, and I have the utmost respect for each and every one. Their collective knowledge has been a constant source of information. Many offered advice and suggestions, and several took their own time to review and proofread the manuscript. To all, I say thank you.

Thank you to Douglas Hardwick for reviewing the chapter concerning the Gordon Pipers. His input regarding one of the great traditions at the Indianapolis Motor Speedway proved to be most beneficial.

Ken Keltner and Lee Ann Cyb of Keltner and Associates representing Herff-Jones provided information regarding the Winner's Ring. A meeting with Ken proved to be not only enlightening but entertaining as well. Thank you, Ken and Lee Ann.

Jeanine Head Miller, curator of domestic life for The Henry Ford in Dearborn, Michigan, could not have been more helpful. She provided the information for chapter 50 "The Quilt Lady." Through phone calls and mail, she provided much-needed advice.

Sabrina List is the vice president for marketing and communication with the 500 Festival. She edited the many sections devoted to the festival. Thank you, Sabrina.

I had the opportunity to speak with Pat Kennedy on the phone and to meet him in person. Pat has authored *The Official Indy 500 Trivia Book* and *Indy 500 Recaps—The Short Chute Edition.* His advice gained through personal experience proved to be invaluable.

I would like to thank Steve Shunck of BorgWarner, Inc., for editing the copy on the chapters on the greatest trophy in sports and the Borg-Warner Wreath.

Thank you to Dawn DeBellis and Joel Wittman in Creatives Services at the Indianapolis Motor Speedway for supplying the Wing and Wheel image.

Mike Roth oversees the Photo Shop at the Indianapolis Motor Speedway. Maintaining more than 5 million images of the speedway and the 500 is a meticulous and time-consuming job. However, every time I visited the shop to select pictures for this publication, he and his staff were always ready to assist and offer advice. Thank you, Mike.

Many thanks to Mark Miles, CEO of Hulman & Company, Doug Boles, president of the Indianapolis Motor Speedway, and C. J. O'Donnell, chief marketing officer for Hulman Motorsports at the time of this writing, for granting permission to use many of the pictures in this publication.

Last, but not least, I would like to thank Ashley Runyon, trade and regional acquisitions editor, Indiana University Press; Rachel Rosolina, project manager/editor, Indiana University Press; David Hulsey, associate director and director of marketing and sales, Indiana University Press; David Miller, lead project manager/editor, Indiana University Press; and Jennifer Crane, editorial project manager, Amnet Systems. These are the people who brought this book to life. I simply supplied words, numbers, and pictures. I could not be more grateful.

THE *INDIANAPOLIS*
500

PART 1

Previous page, The World's Greatest Racecourse

THE INDIANAPOLIS MOTOR SPEEDWAY

The Indianapolis Motor Speedway is about many things. It is about speed and technology. It is about men and women with incredible talent and courage pushing one another and their machines beyond limits once believed unattainable. It is about families making annual pilgrimages to the Great Place. For many it is the only time of year they see one another. It is about memories. It is about renewing old friendships and making new ones, and it is about traditions.

Traditions serve as common threads in the tapestry that is the history of the Indianapolis Motor Speedway, linking the past to the present. Several traditions were born even before the first Indianapolis 500-Mile Race and are honored to this very day. Others originated at various times during the last more than one hundred years with no prior planning. As said by Donald Davidson, track historian at the famed race course, "If you try to plan a tradition, it won't take off, and then some stupid thing will become a huge craze, and it happened by accident."[1] Such is the genesis of most traditions. Through the years some traditions have been modified to suit changing times, while many are still in place in their original form.

Traditions are central to the spirit of the Indianapolis Motor Speedway, and as said by Tony George, chairman of the board, "Its spirit touches all who enter."[2]

1

THE BRICKYARD

THE EARLY 1900S SAW INDIANA EMERGE AS ONE OF THE LEADERS in the brand-new automobile industry. More than fifty manufacturers called Indiana home, and many early-day classics such as Marmon, Cole, National, Stutz, and Duesenberg had their operations based in Indianapolis at one time or another.

There was, however, a problem. Indiana roads were little more than dirt or gravel paths at that time and were still several years away from being paved with either blacktop or concrete. As a result, there was nowhere for manufacturers to test their products. As technology improved, the vehicles became capable of greater speeds than any public road could provide.

"What we need," said one visionary, "is a huge, sprawling speedway at which an automobile could be extended to its fullest in order to find its weakest point . . . then go back and make it better." Additionally, occasional racing events could be conducted to give the manufacturers an opportunity to prove their worth against one another in competition, thereby providing the general public with opportunities to observe and form opinions on what they might consider purchasing for personal use.

That visionary was Carl G. Fisher. He joined forces with Arthur C. Newby, head of the National Motor Vehicle Company; Frank H. Wheeler, president of the Wheeler-Schebler Carburetor Company; and James A. Allison, whose experimental company would eventually grow into the massive Allison Engineering concern, the prolific manufacturer of the Liberty Aircraft Engine.

From left, founding fathers Arthur C. Newby, Frank H. Wheeler, Carl G. Fisher, and James A. Allison.

Founders Arthur C. Newby, Frank H. Wheeler, Carl G. Fisher, and James A. Allison memorialized on the administration building in celebration of the hundredth anniversary of the Indianapolis 500-Mile Race.

The Vision. While on his way to Savannah, Georgia, in March 1909, race car driver Lewis Strang stopped to see a scale model of the new racecourse under construction. Two years later he would start from the pole position in the inaugural 500-Mile Race on May 30, 1911.

In mid-December 1908, four eighty-acre tracts of farmland lying approximately five miles northwest of Indianapolis were purchased by the group. The land had been known by locals as the old Pressley Farm.

The following spring a track began to take shape. Two parallel straightaways, each measuring five-eighths of a mile, and four sweeping turns, each measuring one-quarter of a mile and banked at 9 degrees 12 minutes, were connected to two short straights, each measuring one-eighth of mile, resulting in a complete lap of two and a half miles around.

In early 1909 Carl Fisher founded the Aero Club of Indiana, for which he served as president, and he began taking balloon-piloting lessons from George Bumbaugh. It is believed Fisher was the twenty-first person in the United States to qualify as a balloon pilot. He now envisioned the track as a proving ground not only for automobiles but for aviation as well.

The first race at Indianapolis.

In an effort to promote the new facility, which was still under construction, Fisher outbid several other cities for the right to host the US National Balloon Championships. It would be the first competitive event ever conducted at the Indianapolis Motor Speedway.

On June 5, 1909, nine balloons ascended into the heavens. More than thirty-five thousand people were in attendance, but the vast majority chose not to pay the admission fee, reasoning they could see the greater part of the ascent from outside the track.

The crowd was so large, in fact, Indiana Governor Thomas R. Marshall, who would four years later serve as vice president of the United States, was delayed in his arrival, mired in traffic on Georgetown Pike. Scheduled to be part of the opening ceremony, he did not arrive until shortly before four o'clock in the afternoon. To his dismay, all he saw in the western sky were the first balloons departing.

The championship was won by University City, a St. Louis entry, piloted by John Berry and Paul McCullough. They zigzagged their way 382 miles to Fort Payne, Alabama. Carl Fisher and George Bumbaugh finished fourth.

By August 1909 the track was declared ready for competition. However, an ambitious motorcycle program and three days of automobile racing had to be shortened due to the dreadful track conditions, as the surface began to deteriorate almost immediately. The mixture of crushed rock and tar made it little more than an oiled dirt track, which proved to be unsuitable for racing. Something had to be done!

Hoosier pride!

The first motorized race at Indianapolis.

After much consideration it was determined bricks would provide the most durable surface while being able to withstand the harsh Indiana winters. In the fall of 1909, 3.2 million paving bricks, each weighing approximately nine and a half pounds, arrived by rail from the western part of the state. Although several neighboring firms were subcontracted to fill the enormous requirement, approximately 90 percent of the bricks used were supplied by Culver Blocks and bore the wording "Pat. May 21, 1901," which was the date on which Reuben Culver's patent was granted.

The bricks were laid in a bed of sand on top of the crushed rock and tar and then fixed with mortar. Employing more than two hundred men with mules, wooden carts, and gaslights, the entire project was completed in just sixty-three days, by which time the speedway was already nicknamed the "Brickyard." Approximately 85 percent of the bricks remain today, buried under several layers of asphalt.

With a new racing surface in place in 1909, a most ambitious racing program was announced for 1910. This would include a trio of three-day events of automobile racing over the holiday weekends of Memorial Day, the Fourth of July, and Labor Day; a week-long aviation meet in June, highlighted by the presence of the Wright brothers from Dayton, Ohio; and a twenty-four-hour race on August 12. The latter, however, was canceled on July 4.

The events of Memorial Day weekend were most successful, with a crowd of fifty thousand attending on Memorial Day. With the coming of summer, however, attendance began to drop, and the events of neither the Fourth of July nor Labor Day produced crowds rivaling the size of that seen on Memorial Day. Perhaps, reasoned Fisher, Allison, Wheeler, and Newby, there had been too much racing.

After much discussion management decided only one event would be held in 1911, but it would be of grand proportions and pay a huge purse, with careful consideration given to the needs of the spectators. It was reasoned an event starting at ten o'clock in the morning and lasting six or seven hours would allow ample time for everyone to leave the grounds and be home in time for their evening meals.

Based on these parameters and considering attainable speeds by automobiles at the time, it was determined it would be a five-hundred-mile race.

The original date of May 30, 1911, was chosen after much consideration. Lem Trotter was a close friend and business associate of Carl Fisher. He had, in fact, assisted the four founding fathers in selecting and procuring the land on which the speedway sits. In discussions for selecting the date for the first race, Trotter recommended Memorial Day. He reasoned the plan was to draw spectators far beyond the local farming community. Additionally, a farming procedure known as "haying" took place in late May, and it was followed by a two-week break, thereby allowing farmers the opportunity to attend to other matters, including a five-hundred-mile race.

The matter was settled. The inaugural Indianapolis 500 was contested on May 30, 1911. It was won by Indianapolis resident Ray Harroun in the locally constructed Marmon Wasp. The day was a huge success, with more than eighty thousand fans in attendance. The "Greatest Spectacle in Racing" was born.

Ray Harroun wins the inaugural 500-Mile Race in 1911.

Captain Eddie Rickenbacker.

Since the first Indianapolis 500 in 1911, the race has always been scheduled in conjunction with Memorial Day. For many the race heralds the beginning of summer. From 1911 through 1970 it was conducted on May 30 regardless of the day of the week, with one exception. When May 30 fell on a Sunday, the race was scheduled for May 31, the following Monday.

In 1971 the Uniform Holiday Act took effect, moving Memorial Day from a fixed date of May 30 to a designated Monday, establishing a three-day weekend. Since that time the race has been scheduled for Memorial Day weekend. In 1971 and 1972, the race was scheduled for the Saturday of Memorial Day weekend. In 1973 the race was scheduled for Monday of Memorial Day weekend, but it was delayed until Wednesday due to rain. Since 1974 the race has been scheduled for the Sunday of Memorial Day weekend.

Because of two rainouts, the 1986 race, originally scheduled for May 25, was conducted on Saturday, May 31. In 1997 the race was plagued by two rain delays. Originally scheduled for Sunday, May 25, the race was started the following day, but rain showers resulted in suspending the race on the fifteenth lap. The race resumed the following day under sunny skies, with Arie Luyendyk claiming his second victory.

Returning to the early years of the speedway, we see things were about to change. Frank Wheeler passed in 1921, and by 1927 Arthur Newby was in poor health and had retired from industry, and Fisher and Allison were in the process of pursuing other interests. Fisher would eventually play major roles in the development of Miami Beach, Montauk Point on Long Island, and the first cross-country highway.

On August 31, 1927, World War I flying ace Eddie Rickenbacker, leading a new group, took over ownership of the track. Captain Rickenbacker had in fact driven in the Indianapolis 500 several times before he even learned how to fly an airplane.

Captain Rickenbacker would soon face many challenges, not the least of which was the Great Depression. A persuasive, hands-on leader, he was able to successfully direct the speedway through the perilous 1930s.

During World War II, however, the facility stood silent and fell into a dreadful state of disrepair. Unlike the years during World War I, when the track had been used as a military aviation repair depot and refueling point for military aircraft, maintenance of the facility was virtually nonexistent.

So bad was the state of affairs, many locals believed the track would succumb to housing developers in anticipation of the postwar housing boom.

Enter three-time Indianapolis 500 champion Wilbur Shaw. Shaw fervently tried to assemble a group of investors to save the track, but to no avail. Shaw's friend and associate Homer Cochran suggested he contact a businessman with whom he had dealings in the past. He turned to the grandson of a German immigrant, Anton "Tony" Hulman Jr., of Terre Haute, Indiana. Hulman's wholesale grocery company owned the successful Clabber Girl Baking Powder Company.

Hulman was a proud Hoosier, and he was greatly interested in seeing the Indianapolis 500-Mile Race return to its former glory. Following several visits to the track in quick succession, events proceeded at a rapid pace.

On November 14, 1945, Hulman purchased the Indianapolis Motor Speedway from Captain Eddie Rickenbacker for $750,000 and named Shaw president. Despite the condition of the facility, Hulman vowed the Indianapolis 500-Mile Race would once again be conducted, beginning in 1946. He kept his word.

Hulman passed on October 27, 1977. The speedway could not have had a better steward. Under his leadership the Indianapolis 500-Mile Race became the world's largest single-day sporting event, and the Indianapolis Motor Speedway rightfully assumed the title of the World's Greatest Race Course.

Above, Anton "Tony" Hulman Jr. (left) with Wilbur Shaw.

Left, Anton "Tony" Hulman Jr.

The speedway remains in the Hulman-George family to this day, and the leadership continues to ensure the vision of Anton "Tony" Hulman Jr. is realized.

The Indianapolis Motor Speedway has survived two world wars, the Great Depression, and two ownership changes. Despite all these things, it has endured for more than one hundred years. It remains to this very day, the Brickyard.

The front stretch in 1938.

2

THE YARD OF BRICKS

THE BRICK SURFACE OF THE SPEEDWAY BEGAN TO DETERIORATE IN the turns as the years passed. In the spring of 1936, patches of asphalt were laid over the rougher portions, and more and more asphalt was laid over the next two years. By the time of the 1939 race, only about 650 yards of the main straight were still bricks, and they remained for another twenty-two years.

In October 1961 the remaining bricks were covered, with the exception of a three-foot strip the entire width of the track at the start/finish line in remembrance of the original surface. Since that time, the entire surface has been repaved several times, most recently in 2004. Each time, a fresh batch of the original bricks (harvested from underneath the repaved track through the years as tunnels were constructed) is installed once the new surface has had time to harden.[1]

One of the more endearing traditions, the Yard of Bricks remains to this day, paying homage to the history of the Greatest Race Course in the World.

Facing top, Even a puddle can be beautiful.

Facing bottom, Tony Hulman (left) and Ray Harroun commemorated the fiftieth anniversary of the first Indianapolis 500-Mile Race at the Yard of Bricks in 1961 with a singular brick created for the occasion. In 2011 Mari Hulman-George and four-time winner A. J. Foyt placed a commemorative brick in celebration of the hundredth anniversary of the inaugural Indianapolis 500-Mile Race.

3

THE WING AND WHEEL

THE "WING AND WHEEL" LOGO HAS BEEN SYNONYMOUS WITH THE Indianapolis Motor Speedway since its inception in 1909. The exact origin of the logo is unknown. Some believe the reasoning behind the design was to promote not only wheeled events at the facility but aviation as well. In 1910, at the request of Carl Fisher, the Wright brothers brought several biplanes to the track for an ambitious, week-long exhibition. On June 17 of that year, famed aviator Walter Brookins established a new world record for altitude by soaring to a height of 4,938 feet.

As with most logos, the Wing and Wheel has undergone several revisions throughout the years. The early versions had the wing and wheel facing slightly to the viewer's left and the script was slightly curved. The wheel (tire) was representative of the tires being used at the time.

The newest version faces slightly to the viewer's right, and the script is straight across instead of curved. Additionally, the wheel (tire) is wider with more angular shoulders and more accurately resembles the tires being used today.

For many years the logo has been adorned with the seven racing flags, the meanings of which have remained virtually unchanged for the Indianapolis 500 since 1937. From left to right they are:

- Green: The race has started and/or the course is clear. It is also used for restarts following a yellow or red flag.

- White: One lap to go.

- Blue/Orange: Known as either the "courtesy" or "move over" flag, this is normally shown to a participant who is about to be lapped and who is asked to conduct himself or herself accordingly. There is normally no penalty for failing to heed this flag.

- Checkered: The race is completed.
- Red: Come safely to a complete halt when directed. The race has been stopped due to an incident or rain.
- Black: Shown to an individual—and normally accompanied by the display of an individual's car number on a board—requiring the individual to stop at his or her pit for consultation either due to a rule infraction or because of a potential safety problem with the car.
- Yellow: Slow down because of a caution period and pack up in single file behind the pace car. Although caution periods date back to the very early days, the pace car was not used for this purpose at Indianapolis until 1979.[1]

Recognized around the world, the "Wing and Wheel" has been representative of the Indianapolis Motor Speedway for more than one hundred years, and it continues to be a symbol of the World's Greatest Race Course to this day.

The current Wing and Wheel logo.

4

YELLOW SHIRTS

FROM 1909 UNTIL IMMEDIATELY FOLLOWING WORLD WAR II, THE Indiana National Guard was tasked with providing security at the speedway. After Tony Hulman purchased the facility in November 1945, one of his right-hand men, Joseph Quinn of the Clabber Girl Baking Powder Company, established a board of safety and sought advice and input from major law enforcement agencies.

In 1948 the speedway created its own safety patrol. Members were clothed in long-sleeved, dark-blue uniforms and pith helmets. The helmets of department heads were painted gold, and those of the rank and file were painted silver.

The long-sleeved shirts were made of wool and proved to be uncomfortable not only on hot days but also when soaked with rain. In the early 1970s, some staff members chose to wear more comfortable short-sleeved yellow shirts with golden plastic "bump" helmets on the weekends.

By 1975 the blue uniforms and pith helmets had been replaced with yellow shirts and baseball caps, and the term "Yellow Shirts" came into fashion.[1]

Safety patrol in 1954.

Yellow shirts in 2015.

A lone yellow shirt makes his way to his post. Soon the seats will be filled.

5

THE PAGODA

STANDING AT THE START/FINISH LINE AND LOCATED ON THE INSIDE of the track, a Japanese-style pagoda was erected in time for the third running of the Indianapolis 500-Mile Race. It housed timing and scoring, officials, VIP guests, members of the press, and later a radio broadcast booth.

Because it stood fairly close to the edge of the track, the original structure was replaced for the 1926 race due to safety concerns but the new structure still kept with the style of a pagoda.

In 1956–57 the pagoda was replaced by a master control tower made of glass and steel. Its design was representative of modernism architecture, as it resembled a small skyscraper.

As part of the massive construction project begun in 1998 and completed in 2000, the master control tower was replaced by yet another Japanese-style pagoda. The current structure houses timing and scoring, television and radio broadcast booths, and VIP suites. With ten floors and rising to the height of a thirteen-story building, the pagoda is one of the more recognizable buildings in all of sports and reminds one of a sentinel silently standing guard over the Yard of Bricks.[1]

The pagoda in 1913.

The pagoda in 1926.

The master control tower in 1963.

The pagoda in 2000.

The pagoda on May 29, 2016.

THE INDIANAPOLIS 500

Building Materials
- Cubic yards of concrete: 6,100
- Tons of steel: 1,170
- Square feet of glass: 19,500
- Square feet of translucent panel: 17,855
- Square feet of composite panel: 6,060

Interesting Facts
- Height from ground to roof: 153 feet
- Height from ground to top of flagpole: 199 feet
- Total area: 65,000 square feet
- Stories: 13
- Floors: 10

6

THE SCORING PYLON

THE SPEEDWAY INTRODUCED ITS THIRD-GENERATION, STATE-OF-THE-art scoring pylon on the main straightaway just south of the entrance to Gasoline Alley in the summer of 2014. Manufactured by Panasonic, the new pylon features full LED panels on all four sides and provides improved messaging capabilities, animation, and video.[1]

Interesting Facts
- Erected: 2014
- Display: 5,280 LED panels
- Innovations: full LED panels, improved messaging capabilities, animation, and video

Facing top, Green! Green! Green!

Facing bottom, Only in America!

THE SCORING PYLON

7

FOOD

UNLIKE MANY SPORTING VENUES, THE INDIANAPOLIS MOTOR SPEEDWAY permits spectators to bring their own food and beverages into the facility. There are two requirements, however. No glass containers are permitted, and coolers or containers are limited in size to no larger than 14"×14"×18" so as to fit under the grandstand seats.

Some of the more traditional items available at the concession stands are Indy dogs, Brickyard burgers, and Track fries. The food of choice, however, is the pork tenderloin sandwich. This traditional offering is a midwestern creation and is sold at various concession stands throughout the facility.

Mary Catherine "Mom" Unser, mother of Jerry, Bobby, and Al Sr., was known for her famous spicy chili. From mid-1960s until her passing in 1975, she would annually treat participants to a cookout in the garage area.[1]

MOM UNSER'S LEGENDARY CHILI

Ingredients

- 1 pound lean pork (tenderloin or chops)
- 1 medium onion
- 1 clove fresh garlic
- 1 No. 2 can diced tomatoes
- 3 cups fresh roasted, peeled, and diced green chiles (medium to hot)
- 1 shake dried oregano
- Salt to taste

Preparation

1. Remove all fat from pork and cube. Sauté pork, onion, and garlic together until cooked. Squeeze tomatoes through fingers and add to skillet with juice. Add green chiles, oregano, and salt. Simmer about 35 minutes. Pinto beans may be added if desired, or served as a side dish.

2. To roast fresh green chiles, rinse chiles and place on a hot barbecue rack. Turn chiles until skin is uniformly roasted. Place chiles in a bowl, and cover with a damp dishcloth. (This allows the chiles to "sweat" and the skin to loosen from the meat of the chili). Wait 15 minutes, then begin removing the skins, and remove the stem along with the seed stem. Keep some seeds to add for flavor.

The pork tenderloin sandwich is an Indiana favorite.

8

GASOLINE ALLEY

GASOLINE ALLEY IS A NICKNAME FOR THE GARAGE AREA AT THE
speedway where the cars are housed at race time. It is believed the
permanent garage area at Indianapolis Motor Speedway was the first
of its kind anywhere in the world. Located inside Turn 1, the original
garages were in place by 1910.

In the early years the term Gasoline Alley referred to only one corner
of the garage area where fuel was dispensed. In the 1920s it came to be
applied to the entire complex. The name may have been borrowed from
the cartoon strip "Gasoline Alley," which debuted in August 1919.

Between 1914 and 1915, new garages were constructed in the infield
just south and slightly behind the pagoda. These wooden buildings,
painted white with green trim, became iconic structures at the track
for the next several decades. There is a re-creation of one of the garages
in the Indianapolis Motor Speedway Museum located on the grounds
of the speedway.

In 1986 the wooden garages were razed to make room for new, more
modern concrete structures. There are now three banks of thirty-two
garages capable of housing up to ninety-six cars. Each garage measures
twenty feet wide and twenty-four feet deep, and the area is complete with
restroom and shower facilities for team members.

Two of the four sides (north and east) of the perimeter of the garage
area contain accessory company headquarters. Suppliers including
Simpson Safety, Firestone, Bell Helmets, Honda, Chevrolet, Dallara,
and Lincoln Electric occupy these garages during race events.

Case Garage in 1913.

Above, Gasoline Alley in 1957.

Facing top, Wilbur Shaw (left door opening, center) in his garage following victory in 1937.

Firestone is the official tire supplier to the IndyCar Series. For the hundredth running of the Indianapolis 500-Mile Race, Firestone honored those drivers who won the race on Firestone tires by placing their names on the sidewalls.

E85r fuel powers the IndyCar Series.

A permanent fuel depot is located on the east side of the garage area. Pumps for unleaded fuel for support vehicles and E85r race fuel for the IndyCar Series are available at this location.

Gasoline Alley at dawn.

9

THE INDIANAPOLIS MOTOR SPEEDWAY MUSEUM

THE INDIANAPOLIS MOTOR SPEEDWAY MUSEUM, LOCATED FIVE MILES northwest of downtown Indianapolis on the grounds of the famous Indianapolis Motor Speedway, is recognized as one of the more highly visible museums in the world devoted to automobiles and auto racing. In 1987 the speedway grounds were honored with the designation of National Historic Landmark.

Tony Hulman and Karl Kizer, the museum's first director, established the original Indianapolis Motor Speedway Museum in 1956. The building was located at the southwest corner of the speedway's property where the speedway's administration building now stands. It was only large enough to display a few vintage race cars. It soon became obvious something more substantial was needed.

In 1975 Hulman built a larger, more modern museum within the speedway oval, and its opening coincided with the United States' Bicentennial Celebration in 1976.

Constructed of precast cement and Wyoming quartz, the facility encompasses 96,000 square feet of display and administrative office space. Museum display space measures approximately 37,500 square feet. A glass canopy above the main display floor provides year-round natural light. The building also houses two speedway gift shops, the track's photography department, and museum staff offices.

The departure area for bus tours of the historic two-and-a-half-mile oval is located near the museum's front doors.

About one-fifth of the estimated 160,000 visitors who tour the museum annually do so in May, the month of the Indianapolis 500-Mile Race.

Above, The original museum in 1965.

Below, The new museum opened in 1976.

- The museum is open 363 days a year (closed Thanksgiving Day and Christmas Day).
- Open: 9:00 a.m.–5:00 p.m. (ET) March to October.
- 10:00 a.m.–4:00 p.m. (ET) November to February.
- Note: Indianapolis is in the Eastern time zone.
- The museum has extended hours during race events.
- For more information, contact the museum welcome desk at (317) 492-6784. Information on the museum's hours, operations, collections, and displays are provided at www.indyracingmuseum.org.

LOCATION

The museum is located inside the track between Turns 1 and 2. The entrance to the Museum is located at Gate 2 on Sixteenth Street.

Approximately seventy-five vehicles and featured attractions are on display at any one time, including the following possibilities:

- The Marmon "Wasp," which won the inaugural Indianapolis 500 in 1911 with Ray Harroun at the wheel and was featured on a postage stamp in the US Postal Service's Transportation Series
- Four two-time winning cars: the Boyle Maserati (Wilbur Shaw 1939–40); the Blue Crown Spark Plug Special (Mauri Rose 1947–48); the Fuel Injection Special (Bill Vukovich 1953–54); and the Belond Special (Sam Hanks 1957 and Jimmy Bryan 1958)
- More than thirty Indianapolis 500-winning cars
- The four cars driven to victory by A. J. Foyt Jr., including his 1977 machine that represents his record-setting fourth Indianapolis 500 win
- The Duesenberg #12 Murphy Special, the only car ever to win both Indianapolis 500 (1922) and the French Grand Prix at Le Mans (1921)

- Dave Evans's #8 Cummins Diesel Special, the first car to complete the Indianapolis 500 without a pit stop, in 1931
- The 1965 Le Mans-winning Ferrari 250 LM
- A 1954/55 Mercedes-Benz Formula One car
- A 1957 SSI Corvette
- A rare 1935 Duesenberg Model JN four-door convertible passenger car, of which only three were built
- An equally rare 1925 McFarlan TV6 passenger roadster

From time to time the Indianapolis Motor Speedway Museum will feature certain "themed" cars, owners, and drivers of the Indianapolis 500-Mile Race.

The museum has an extensive trophy collection, including the famed Borg-Warner Trophy, which honors the winner of each Indianapolis 500, along with auto racing trophies, honors, and awards from around the world.

For a more visual taste of the Indianapolis 500, the museum offers visitors the Tony Hulman Theatre, featuring a presentation of rare historic footage and Indianapolis 500 highlights. Outside the museum, visitors can see the Louis Chevrolet Memorial, featuring a bronze bust of Chevrolet with four bronze panels about his automotive accomplishments, a limestone sculpture of a Novi open-wheel race car, and a limestone sculpture of an A. J. Foyt Coyote race car.

TRACK TOURS

Track tours (one lap on the two-and-a-half-mile oval track in an IMS bus, narrated) are available any day except when there is racing, testing, special events, construction, or winter weather conditions.

GROUNDS TOURS

The one-and-a-half-hour narrated tour of this historic facility gives guests the opportunity to tour the oval track, the media center, the pagoda, the victory podium, the garage area, and a Gasoline Alley Suite, plus stand on the famous Yard of Bricks at the start/finish line. In addition, guests tour the Indianapolis Motor Speedway Museum. Special arrangements may be made for group tours (minimum of 20).[1]

The Tony Hulman Theatre features rare historic footage and highlights the Indianapolis 500-Mile Race through the years.

Winning cars of the Indianapolis 500-Mile Race.

Take a lap around this historic racetrack in one of the museum's tour buses.

10

FORE!

THE BRICKYARD CROSSING GOLF COURSE IS LOCATED ON THE grounds of the Indianapolis Motor Speedway. The original eighteen-hole layout was designed by Bill Diddle in 1929 at the request of then-owner Captain Eddie Rickenbacker. Nine holes were located  outside the track, and the nine holes located inside were accessible by a wooden bridge that spanned the brick-paved speedway. In 1965 nine holes were added to the nine holes outside, bringing the total to twenty-seven holes. The course is believed to be the first automobile race track golf course in the United States.

For several years the course played host to the PGA Tour in May as a prelude to the Indianapolis 500. A favorite for players and fans alike, the 500 Festival Open was conducted from 1960 to 1964 and again from 1966 to 1968.

In 1991 there was a need for more of the infield for the track's infrastructure. Famed golf course architect and Indiana resident Pete Dye was hired to redesign the course. The original course was demolished, and the number of holes was reduced from twenty-seven to eighteen, with fourteen holes outside the track and four holes inside the famed oval. Access to the inside four holes is now by way of a tunnel running under the track.

The project took two years to complete. During that time the track's internal safety barrier, consisting of a concrete and rebar wall about four feet high, two feet thick, and two and a half miles long, was replaced. Officials were faced with the prospect of needing to crush the material and having the rubble removed at considerable cost. Dye was asked if any of the material could be used on the remodeled course. After surveying a section of wall that had been crushed and prepared for removal, he inquired as to the weight of the rubble. Pleased with the response, he quickly announced, "I'll take it all." Today that material lines both sides of the creek that runs throughout the fourteen holes outside the track.

From 1994 to 2000, the Senior Tour made stops at the famed layout. In September 2017 the LPGA made its first appearance at the Brickyard, and the facility received great reviews by players, officials, and fans alike.

The Brickyard Crossing Golf Course is open to the public, and it is expertly maintained. It provides a stern challenge for the most accomplished golfer while offering an enjoyable experience for the higher-handicapped player, with views unlike any other golf course in the world—the Indianapolis Motor Speedway.[1]

Facing, The Brickyard Crossing Golf Course.

Below, Golfers are treated to exciting views during a round on this challenging course.

11

DONALD DAVIDSON

DONALD DAVIDSON IS THE HISTORIAN AT THE INDIANAPOLIS MOTOR Speedway. As a child growing up in England, he became obsessed with the "500" and memorized an abundance of facts and historical details about the race and its participants. As a young adult, his dream of one day attending the great race was realized when he travelled to America in 1964. Armed with the knowledge he had acquired at such a young age, he was immediately accepted by the racing community and quickly accepted into its inner circle.

In 1965 he returned to the United States, this time he carrying only a one-way ticket and a green card. IMS Radio Network chief announcer Sid Collins asked him to serve as a commentator on the race-day broadcast, and Davidson never looked back. It is a duty he has performed ever since.

Director of Competition Henry Banks was so impressed by the young man he hired him a week after the race to be the keeper of records for the United States Auto Club, the sanctioning body of the 500 at that time.

Since 1965 Davidson has contributed to dozens of books, written many stories and articles for magazines and local newspapers, presented hundreds of talks, been a featured guest on ABC News, and made appearances on CBS, NBC, and CNN. His book with Rick Shaffer, titled *Autocourse Official History of the Indianapolis 500*, is considered to be the definitive work on the subject. [1]

Donald Davidson.

Since 1971 Davidson has hosted a call-in radio program every May, and for more than thirty years he has conducted a four-night course on the history of the 500 at IUPUI, the Indianapolis-based campus of Purdue and Indiana Universities.

On January 1, 1998, Davidson joined the staff at the Indianapolis Motor Speedway. He can frequently be seen in the Indianapolis Motor Speedway Museum in conversations with guests, amazing them by being able to recall even the slightest detail of every race.

He was inducted into the Auto Racing Hall of Fame in 2010 and the Indiana Broadcast Pioneers Hall of Fame in 2013.

Davidson has been told he has a "selective retentive easy access memory." He has the ability to memorize that which is most important to him with the greatest detail. It is a gift that has served him well.

12

TOM CARNEGIE

TOM CARNEGIE WAS A YOUNG BROADCASTER WHO KNEW NOTHING about auto racing when he started as track announcer at the Indianapolis Motor Speedway in 1946, where he stayed until his retirement in 2006.

Carnegie was born on September 25, 1919, in Norwalk, Connecticut, the son of a Baptist minister. During his childhood his family moved from Connecticut to Waterloo, Iowa, then to Pontiac, Michigan, and finally to Kansas City, Missouri.

Carnegie attended William Jewell College in Liberty, Missouri, where he was a baseball player. During his junior year he was diagnosed with a "polio type" illness which led to partial paralysis in one of his legs. The affliction ended his baseball career and led to him entering extemporaneous speech and debate competitions. It was not long before he became a star debater. One of the competitions he won was a sports radio contest.

After graduating in 1942 he took a job at radio station WOWO in Fort Wayne, Indiana, where he served as an announcer for the Fort Wayne Pistons basketball team. It was at this time he started using "Tom Carnegie" instead of his given name Carl Kenagy—his station manager though it sounded better. He would later take a job in Indianapolis, Indiana, at radio station WIRE.[1]

Carnegie credited a young Ronald Reagan with being a major influence on his broadcast aspirations. While living in Waterloo, Iowa, he would regularly listen to Reagan's radio broadcasts.

One of his jobs in Indianapolis was that of announcing antique car shows. In 1946 at one of the shows, Carnegie was approached by Tony Hulman, the new owner of the Indianapolis Motor Speedway, who

Tom Carnegie.

offered him a position as PA announcer at the speedway. It was an opportunity Carnegie enthusiastically accepted. For the next sixty-one years he would announce races and become known as the "voice of the speedway."

Carnegie is probably best known for two signature phrases. When a driver entered the front stretch at the beginning of a qualifying run, one could hear him fervently say, "Aaaaaaaad heeeeeeee's ON IT!" Following the setting of a new track record, Carnegie would passionately announce, "Race fans, you're not going to believe this. It's a neeeeeeeew traaaaaaaack record!" Those calls are forever in the memories of those who were fortunate to hear them.[2]

During his tenure at the speedway, Carnegie served as the sports director for WRTV, originally WFBM-TV, in Indianapolis from 1953 until he retired from the position in 1985. During this time he also served as the PA announcer for the Indiana State High School Basketball Championships. He portrayed the PA announcer at the championship game at historic Hinkle Fieldhouse on the campus of Butler University in the film *Hoosiers*.[3]

Tom Carnegie passed on February 11, 2011, at the age of ninety-one. During his career at the speedway he called sixty-one Indianapolis 500s, twelve Brickyard 400s, and six United States Grands Prix.

Below are interesting facts about Tom Carnegie as compiled by Indianapolis Motor Speedway historian Donald Davidson:

- Tom Carnegie called sixty-one of the first ninety-four Indianapolis 500-Mile Races, nearly two-thirds of the number of races since the event began in 1911.
- There were eleven presidents of the United States during Tom Carnegie's tenure as IMS public address announcer. When he called his first 500 in 1946, Harry Truman was president. Former presidents Bill Clinton and George W. Bush, both of whom occupied the Oval Office during Carnegie's tenure, were not alive in 1946.
- Of the 708 different drivers who started in an Indianapolis 500 through 2006, 411 of them made their debut with Tom Carnegie on the public address.
- Every grandstand or building seen from inside IMS was built after Tom Carnegie started his public address tenure in 1946.
- While some buildings outside the track are older, it is believed the oldest structure one can now see from inside the track is the Emergency Medical Center, built in 1948, and operated by Indiana University Health.
- The single-lap record when Tom Carnegie debuted in 1946 was Ralph Hepburn's 134.449 mph. Fifty years later, Arie Luyendyk recorded one at 237.498 mph, thus exceeding Hepburn's speed by 103 mph. Carnegie called both attempts.

- The low end of prize money in 2006, Tom Carnegie's final year, was Larry Foyt's $192,305 for thirtieth place. In 1946, Carnegie's first year, the entire purse was $115,679, and Hal Cole's portion for thirty-second was $600.

- A. J. Foyt drove in the 500 a record thirty-five consecutive times between 1958 and 1992. Tom Carnegie called twelve races before Foyt even arrived and another fourteen after his last start.

- When Tom Carnegie first called the 500 in 1946, there were only five radio stations in town and no television stations.

- At least twenty-two drivers Tom Carnegie called on race day have been the sons, grandsons, or nephews of a driver who had previously competed during his tenure.

- The last time fans heard Tom Carnegie bellow his famous phrase, "It's a neeeeeeeew traaaaaaaack record!" came during Arie Luyendyk's assault on the record books on May 12, 1996. On May 12, 1984, Carnegie said it five times in less than three minutes. Luyendyk broke the track record on his opening qualifying lap with a speed of 237.498 mph and topped it on each succeeding lap, shattering the four-lap mark in the process with an average of 236.986 mph.[4]

Facing, May is a magical month for fans of all ages.

PART 2

THE *MONTH* OF *MAY*

May is a magical month for the citizens of Indiana and race fans around the world. For more than one hundred years, it has been the month of the Indianapolis 500-Mile Race. For millions of fans, May is met with the same eager anticipation as that of a small child awaiting the arrival of Santa Claus on Christmas Eve.

The anticipation begins to accelerate when the track opens for the first day of practice, and it builds to a crescendo with the command to start the engines. There are parties, concerts, parades, and other numerous events throughout the month. And then there is race day and the prerace festivities where pageantry and tradition intertwine, providing an experience unlike any other in all of sports.

It simply must be experienced to be understood.

Mr. First in Line.

13

"MR. FIRST IN LINE"

FOR THIRTY-SEVEN STRAIGHT YEARS, HE WAS FIRST IN LINE WHEN the gates at the speedway opened for practice in early May. A mechanic from Yuma, Arizona, Lawrence "Larry" Bisceglia became infatuated with the Indianapolis 500 when he first attended the race in 1926.

In 1948 he set a goal of being the first in line on opening day, but when he arrived at the main gate in his 1933 DeSoto, he was surprised to see two cars ahead of him. He left a few days earlier in 1949 but was still beaten to the gate yet again by one vehicle. In 1950 he reached his goal.

In 1955 he acquired a 1951 Chevrolet panel truck he adorned with racing decals.

In 1958 the speedway gave him a lifetime pass to the race, and Tony Hulman awarded him with a key to the speedway gates. An electrical outlet was installed outside the track so he could use small appliances to ease his stay.

On Pole Day in 1967, Bisceglia was called to the start/finish line, where Hulman presented him with a new Ford Econoline on behalf of the Ford Motor Company. The old Chevrolet panel truck was donated to the Indianapolis Motor Speedway Museum, where it still resides.

Bisceglia drove to the speedway for the last time in 1983 as his health began to fail. He was still able to be first in line through 1985, but how he was able to make the trip is unknown.

He did not make opening day in 1986, and it appeared he would miss the race as well. When he was located in Yuma, Arizona, where he had been living in a van on a friend's business parking lot, several offers came pouring in to fly him to the race. Mario Andretti led a group of drivers by donating $100 to the cause.

Bisceglia attended his last race in 1987. On December 7, 1988, "Mr. First in Line" passed. He will always be remembered as more than a spectator.[1]

14

ELEVEN ROWS OF THREE

FORTY-SIX ENTRIES WERE RECEIVED FOR THE INAUGURAL INDIANAPOLIS 500. Of those, two failed to make it to the track due to a lack of parts.

A requirement of achieving a speed of 75 mph over one-quarter mile distance down the front straightaway from a flying start was imposed. Forty cars met the minimum and would start the race.

Following the inaugural race, the contest board of the American Automobile Association (AAA)—the sanctioning body—and founder Carl Fisher questioned the number of starters in the interest of safety. Were there too many? Should there be more? Was the number just right? The AAA was tasked with determining the right number. It was decided a safe distance between each car spread equally around the course would be four hundred feet. With a track distance of 2.5 miles, the number of starters was determined to be thirty-three (13,200 feet/400 feet = 33). Fisher, however, imposed a limit of thirty cars between 1912 and 1914.

Between 1912 and 1928 the field was not filled. The allowable number was increased during the Depression years (1930–1932) to forty cars (only thirty-eight made it in 1930) and expanded to forty-two in 1933. The maximum number has been thirty-three since 1934 except in 1947, when only thirty cars took the green flag,[1] and in 1979 and 1997, when thirty-five were permitted due to extenuating circumstances.

In 1979 the field was expanded to thirty-five cars to accommodate entries from CART (Championship Auto Racing Teams) and in 1997 to accommodate Lyn St. James and Johnny Unser as they were not guaranteed staring positions due to the fact they were not in the top twenty-five in series' points. Their speeds were among the fastest thirty-three, however, and thus the field was expanded.

The number thirty-three has become a sacred number at the speedway. The water feature in front of the museum has thirty-three small fountains aligned in eleven rows of three surrounding a large singular fountain to represent configuration of the starting field at the drop of the green flag. (The water feature can be seen in the photograph at the bottom of page 41.)

The front row in 2016. From left to right: #28 Ryan Hunter-Reay,
#21 Josef Newgarden, and #5 James Hinchcliffe.

15

QUALIFICATIONS

NUMEROUS QUALIFICATION PROCEDURES HAVE BEEN EMPLOYED throughout the years. As speeds increased and the crowds grew larger, various modifications and enhancements were made in the interest of safety, fan enjoyment, and ensuring only the fastest cars entered would be in the race. Although certain elements of earlier procedures have long since passed, others have remained for decades and are still used to this day.

In 1911 the field was set according to the dates on which entries were received. The first entrant of forty-six received was that of Lewis Strang, and he was awarded the pole. There was, however, one requirement. A driver had to demonstrate he could average 75 mph or better from a flying start over a distance of one-quarter mile. Forty of the forty-six entrants eventually qualified for the race.

In 1912 cars were started according to entry order, but this year drivers were required to average 75 mph for a full lap.

To determine starting positions in 1913 and 1914, a blind draw was employed.

The starting lineup in 1915 was determined by speed with the fastest qualifying car starting on the pole.

To discourage participants from waiting until the last possible moment to qualify, in 1916 an incentive was instituted that remains in place to this day. Single-lap qualifying was still used, but cars would now be positioned according to the day on which they qualified. According to speed, those who qualified on day one would be placed ahead of those who qualified on day two, and so on and so on.

Four-lap qualifications were implemented in 1920 for the first time, and more than one car was permitted on the track at the same time.

From 1933 to 1938, qualifying runs were increased from four laps to ten laps. In 1939 qualifying attempts were changed back to four laps. This tradition remains in place to the present day.

For many decades four days of qualifications, or time trials, were scheduled to include the weekends two weeks prior to the race. The fastest driver on day one was awarded the highly coveted pole position.

From 1998 to 2000 and again from 2010 to 2013, qualifications were limited to the weekend before the race in the interest of cost reduction.

QUALIFYING PROCEDURES, 2010–2013

- A car was permitted one out-lap and one warm-up lap before commencing a qualifying attempt.
- A team member, often the team owner, must wave a green flag signifying an attempt. Otherwise, the attempt will be waived off.
- During any of the four laps, the driver, team owner, or race officials can abort the attempt.
- If the attempt has been started and then terminated, it counts toward the three-attempt limit. If a previous time has been set, it is then forfeited.

Day 1—Pole Day

- Positions 1–24 were open for qualification.
- At day's end, the nine fastest drivers returned for a ninety-minute "shootout" to requalify for the top nine spots, including the pole position.

Day 2—Bump Day

- Positions 25–33 were filled.

- Bumping began once the field was filled.
- Regardless of the day it was qualified, the slowest car in the field was "on the bubble."

Procedures

- Qualification sessions began at noon local time.
- A random draw set the qualifying order for first attempts.
- The session was concluded at 4:00 p.m. Any driver on the track at that time could complete his or her attempt.

QUALIFYING PROCEDURES, 2014–PRESENT

- The grid consists of eleven rows, three cars wide.
- There are two days of qualifying. (Qualifying is also known as time trials.)
- Each driver must put together four good laps around the track (ten miles), and his or her time is used to determine starting position in the race.
- Each driver has the track to himself or herself during qualifying attempts.
- A blind draw is held the day before qualifying to decide in which order the drivers will qualify.
- If no drivers want to qualify during a period, the track will open for practice.
- Each car is permitted two warm-up laps prior to the timed qualification laps. IndyCar Series officials may permit three warm-up laps if they deem the third necessary.
- Practice sessions before time trials commence are scheduled both days.

Day 1 of Qualifying—Saturday

- The thirty-three fastest race cars qualify for the race, but not starting positions (11:00 a.m.–5:50 p.m. ET).
- Any slower cars outside the thirty-three fastest are now out of contention for the race.
- The nine fastest cars earn the right to compete in the shootout the following day.

Day 2 of Qualifying—Sunday (Bump Day)

- The previous day's times are erased.
- Entries 10 through 33 will complete another four-lap qualifying attempt to determine their starting positions (10:15 a.m.–1:30 p.m. ET).
- Drivers qualifying on the second day (Bump Day) are aligned behind the first-day qualifiers even if their speeds are faster than those from the first day.
- Once the field of thirty-three is filled, the slowest car, regardless of the day it qualified, is said to be "on the bubble."
- If another car qualifies faster than the car on the bubble, then it will bump the slower car from the field.
- Shootout: Finally, the fastest nine drivers from Saturday will make one four-lap attempt to determine the pole winner and top three rows (2:00–2:45 p.m. ET).
- Last Row Shootout: In 2015 the slower four entries participated in a forty-five-minute shootout to determine the final three starters.[1]

16

CARB DAY

CARB DAY, FORMERLY KNOWN AS CARBURETION DAY, IS A DAY SET aside to provide one final practice session before the race. On Carb Day cars are configured in "race day trim," as opposed to the less economical configurations used during previous practice sessions for out-and-out speed for qualifications. In the past teams would use much of this time to adjust carburetors, hence its name. In the 1940s fuel injection was introduced as an option, thereby negating the need for carburetors. The name Carb Day remained, however, and it is used to this day. The last cars to use carburetors were the stock-block Ford-powered Lotus machines of Jim Clark and Dan Gurney in 1963.[1]

In recent years Carb Day has been the Friday before the race, held in conjunction with the Freedom 100-Mile Race for the Indy Lights Series, a pit-stop competition, and a concert featuring popular recording artists.

A pit-stop competition has been held on Carb Day since 1977. A fan-favorite, the contest features four rounds of pit-stop action involving twelve teams. During each round, a team will change four tires and simulate a fuel hookup. The quicker time determines the winner in head-to-head competition with time penalties added for various rule infractions such as loose wheel nuts or running over air hoses.

The event is a favorite for crews, as bragging rights and $50,000 go to the winning team.[2] Team Penske has won the contest a record seventeen times. Three-time Indianapolis 500 winner Helio Castroneves leads all drivers with eight titles, all with Team Penske. His most recent victory came on May 27, 2016.[3]

Get ready! Get set! Go!

17

CONCERTS

SINCE 1998 MUSICAL PERFORMANCES HAVE PLAYED A PROMINENT role in the month-long festivities leading up to race day. A concert on Carb Day featuring a top act or acts is held annually with thousands of fans in attendance. Some of the more recent performers have been Kid Rock, Stone Temple Pilots, 3 Doors Down, ZZ Top, Staind and Papa Roach, Lynyrd Skynyrd, and Poison. Kenny Brack, the 1999 Indianapolis 500 champion, performed in 2004 with his group Kenny Brack and the Subwoofers, opening for Live. Additionally, numerous local bands and smaller acts have performed during the month on days featuring on-track activities.

Sammy Hagar and the Wabos and Sublime with Rome headlined the Carb Day activities in 2014. A second headline concert was added the Saturday evening before the race with Jason Aldean performing before a crowd estimated at more than forty thousand fans.[1]

Prior to the hundredth running of the Indianapolis 500-Mile Race in 2016, Journey performed before tens of thousands of fans ready to rock 'n' roll on Carb Day afternoon.

In 2017 the Steve Miller Band and Barenaked Ladies took to the stage, and in 2018 the honor went to Train and Blues Traveler.

Party time!

18

THE LAST ROW PARTY

THE LAST ROW PARTY, A CHARITABLE EVENT, HAS BEEN CONDUCTED since 1972 on the Friday before the race. Organized by the Indianapolis Press Club, it serves as a "roast" for the final three qualifiers for the 500 who will be starting on the eleventh row. Because of the complexities of the qualifying procedures, these three drivers are generally the slowest three in the field, but not always.

Many of these drivers are not well-known, but former and eventual winners have participated in the festivities at some time during their careers. Former winners from the Last Row Party have included Tony Kanaan, Ryan Hunter-Reay, and Buddy Lazier.

Drivers are presented with various gifts, including a special jacket and checks for thirty-one cents, thirty-two cents, and thirty-three cents respectively.

A media figure usually serves as emcee for the event. Over the years this has included Bob Jenkins, Robin Miller, Jack Arute, Dave Wilson, and Laura Steele.

The event was not held in 2013, but the Press Club Foundation conducted a ceremony during the Indy Lights Freedom 100 practice and qualifying day for the honorees. The event returned in 2014.[1]

19

PUBLIC DRIVERS' MEETING

THE DAY BEFORE THE RACE A PUBLIC DRIVERS' MEETING IS HELD ON the front straightaway. This tradition dates back several decades. Open to the public, it is attended by thousands of adoring fans.

All thirty-three starting drivers are in attendance along with celebrities, guests, and presenters. Drivers are seated in ceremonial rows of three; should a driver be unable to attend, a member of the team or family member will take his or her place.

The Public Drivers' Meeting is a time to celebrate achievements. Qualifying awards are handed out and lifetime achievement awards are given. Additionally, trophies from the previous year's race, such as the "Baby Borg," the miniature of the Borg-Warner Trophy, are presented.[1]

Notables in attendance are introduced; some may offer a few remarks. Each of the thirty-three starters is presented with a starter's ring and a race official typically concludes the meeting with final instructions and rules regarding the race.

This event should not be confused with the official drivers' meeting, which is held the morning of the race. That meeting is for race officials and drivers only. It is not open to the public or media.[2]

Following the event drivers are whisked away to downtown Indianapolis where they participate in the 500 Festival Parade with their loved ones.

20

LEGENDS' DAY

SINCE 1998 VARIOUS CEREMONIES, ACTIVITIES, AND FESTIVITIES have been conducted to honor former drivers. In years past, an Indy legend would be honored during the week before the race, and in other years opening day was utilized.

Over time, activities the day before the race were expanded to include an autograph session with all thirty-three starting drivers as well as former drivers, question-and-answer sessions, car displays, a FanFest midway, and a memorabilia show. Starting in 2011 these events held the day before the race have been officially called Legends' Day and feature a designated honoree or honorees.

In 1998 the Parade of Champions included Parnelli Jones, Bobby Unser, Gordon Johncock, Johnny Rutherford, Al Unser Sr., and Tom Sneva.

In 1999 the Legends of the Speedway included Rodger Ward, A. J. Watson, Johnny Rutherford, Jim Rathmann, and Lloyd Ruby.

The 2000 Legends of the Speedway included Joe Leonard, Duke Nalon, Emerson Fittipaldi, Rick Mears, Mario Andretti, and Andy Granatelli.

Cars were honored in 2001 during the Salute to Cars. Indianapolis 500–winning cars from 1911, 1922, 1931, 1951, and 1961 were on display, along with the 1968 Wedge Turbine.

Back-to-back winners Wilbur Shaw, Mauri Rose, Bill Vukovich, Al Unser Sr., and Helio Castroneves were celebrated in 2003.

Additional honorees have included the following:

> 2006: Andretti Opening Day honoring three generations of the Andretti racing family (Mario, Michael, and Marco)

2007: A. J. Foyt Opening Day honoring A. J. Foyt for his fiftieth year of participation

2008: Unser Opening Day honoring the Unser racing family, including Al Unser Sr., Al Unser Jr., Robby Unser, Johnny Unser, and Al Unser III

2011: Legends' Day with A. J. Foyt

2012: Legends' Day with Roger Penske

2013: Legends' Day with Parnelli Jones

2014: Legends' Day with Mario Andretti

2015: Legends' Day with Al Unser Sr.

2016: Legends' Day honoring Champions of the 500

2017: Legends' Day honoring Rookie Winners of the 500

2018: Legends' Day-honoring the roadster era[1]

21

THE 500 FESTIVAL

NO OTHER SINGULAR SPORTING EVENT IN THE WORLD HAS A LEGACY like the Indianapolis 500. No other event has shaped and defined a city and state and their people like the Indianapolis 500.

The 500 Festival, a not-for-profit volunteer organization, was created in 1957 by four forward-thinking civic leaders who wanted to organize a series of events to connect the community to the significance of the Indianapolis 500.

The parade was the 500 Festival's first event back in 1957. That first year more than one hundred fifty thousand spectators lined the parade route, and all nine thousand reserved chair seats were full. Just as today, the Boy Scouts handled seating. Indianapolis Power and Light Company (IPL) had a float in that parade. All these years later, the 500 Festival has never missed a year holding the parade, and IPL has been involved every year as well.

Later that first evening in 1957, more than five hundred people danced to Woody Herman's Orchestra on the fifth floor of the Indiana Roof Ballroom for the Governor's Ball. Tickets to the gala were five dollars a couple. More than sixty years later, this event continues under the name Snakepit Ball.

At the end of June 1957, festival organizers met to debrief and began planning for the next year's festival. Their mission was to create a bigger and better event in 1958. This devotion and diligence set the spirit and speed for every 500 Festival since. More than sixty years later, the 500 Festival has grown to become one of the larger festivals in the nation—leading to new traditions and added economic impact—which further enhances all the benefits of being home to the Indianapolis Motor Speedway.[1]

Each year, more than five hundred thousand Hoosiers and visitors participate in 500 Festival activities throughout the month of May. Among these events are the state's largest health initiative and the nation's premiere half marathon, the OneAmerica 500 Festival Mini-Marathon, and the IPL 500 Festival Parade, one of the nation's premier parades and a more than sixty-year Indianapolis tradition. These events create an exciting and impactful community-led road to the Indianapolis 500.

Throughout the 500 Festival's history, four people have had an instrumental role in shaping it into the organization is it today.

In 1963 the 500 Festival named Josephine Hauck as executive secretary. Hauck was later named executive director. Over the next three decades Hauck transformed the organization into one of the great festivals in the nation. Elizabeth Kraft (Meek) was named president of the 500 Festival in 1992. Her tenure at the festival yielded much change and progress. She worked to modernize the staff's infrastructure and provided the necessary tools and resources for the event business.

In 2003 the 500 Festival board of directors named Kirk Hendrix as its president and CEO. Hendrix brought over twenty-five years of marketing and events experience. Hendrix worked to increase sponsorship and attendance and further develop programming within current events. He has also worked to activate and engage the 500 Festival Foundation, enlisting support of past chairmen and board members.

In 2013 the 500 Festival hired Bob Bryant as its fourth president and CEO. Bryant brings twenty years of experience creating brand-defining successes and significant revenue growth in categories including events, sports, broadcast, motorsports, entertainment, consumer products, retail, and online merchandise store. Bryant has worked to deepen the organization's engagement within the community, leading the launch of the KidsFit Program and the initiative to provide each 500 Festival Princess with a scholarship.

The 500 Festival includes several events.

ONEAMERICA 500 FESTIVAL MINI-MARATHON

The year 2016 marked the fortieth running of the 500 Festival Mini-Marathon. It is one of the nation's larger half marathons with more than thirty-five thousand participants. The race draws US Olympic marathon

Down the stretch they go!

runners, international runners, and families, providing competition and camaraderie.

Starting near the intersection of Washington and West Streets in downtown Indianapolis, the course heads west toward the Indianapolis Motor Speedway along Michigan Street, does one complete lap around the track, and then returns to the finish line down New York Street.

IPL 500 FESTIVAL PARADE

One of the inaugural 500 Festival events, the IPL 500 Festival Parade is one of the nation's premier parades. More than three hundred thousand spectators line the two-mile parade route to experience the larger-than-life floats, giant helium balloons, celebrities, marching bands, patriotic units, and specialty units that fill the streets of

Giants roam the streets!

downtown Indianapolis. The tradition continues with the thirty-three starting drivers of the Indianapolis 500 serving as honorary grand marshals.

The IPL 500 Festival Parade consistently earns national acclaim, ranking as one of the top parades, alongside the Pasadena Tournament of Roses Parade and the Macy's Thanksgiving Day Parade.

The BorgWarner float.

The first year, both the parade and the ball were held on the same evening at 7:00 p.m. the night before the race. Units of the parade included nearly every high school band in the Indianapolis area, the Purdue University Marching Band, various marching units and clowns from the Murat Temple, the Indianapolis Police Department Motorcycle Drill Team, the Culver Military Academy Black Horse Troop, marchers from the Guard's 38th Division and other local military organizations, twenty floats, and all thirty-three starting drivers. Actress Cyd Charisse, wrapped in ermine, and Hugh O'Brien, television's Wyatt Earp, perched on the backs of convertibles and waved to a crowd of more than one hundred-fifty thousand people who lined the parade route.

Today's parade comprises more than eighty entries, including celebrities, race car drivers, floats, bands, balloons, and special units. The journey that started with a handful of civic-minded individuals has created a history that all Hoosiers can look back on with pride, a sense of involvement, and a feeling of community accomplishment.

THE 500 FESTIVAL BREAKFAST AT THE BRICKYARD

Breakfast at the Brickyard, presented by Midwestern Engineers, Inc., is typically held the Saturday of qualifications at the Plaza Pavilion at the Indianapolis Motor Speedway. Open to the public, the event features a hearty Hoosier breakfast and celebrities, dignitaries, and racing legends.

CHASE 500 FESTIVAL KIDS' DAY

Kids' Day is Indiana's largest free outdoor festival for children. The event is held at Monument Circle in downtown Indianapolis and includes mini-car racing, race-themed arts, games, face painting, clowns, mascots, entertainment, and much more. Children ages three to ten are invited to participate in the Chase 500 Festival Rookie Run, a noncompetitive fun run with prizes for all.

THE 500 FESTIVAL MEMORIAL SERVICE

In the midst of all the festivities during the month of May, the 500 Festival's Memorial Service, presented by Rolls-Royce, remembers those Hoosiers who perished while serving in the armed forces. The service includes a joint service color guard presentation of colors, various musical performances, and a wreath-laying ceremony. A horse-drawn caisson and a caparisoned horse trails behind with boots reversed in the stirrups, representing a leader who has fallen and will ride no more. The service takes place at the Indiana War Memorial in downtown Indianapolis.

KEYBANK 500 FESTIVAL SNAKEPIT BALL

The KeyBank 500 Festival Snakepit Ball is a legendary race-weekend party in Indianapolis. Boasting an eclectic crowd of business and civic leaders, coupled with celebrities and VIPs in town for the Indianapolis 500, the Snakepit Ball experience is like no other event. Celebrity red-carpet arrivals are a highlight of this popular black-tie event.

THE 500 FESTIVAL AND INDIANAPOLIS 500 EDUCATION PROGRAM

This award-winning program for Indiana fourth-grade students, presented by Indiana University Health, opens up the world of the 500 Festival and

Indianapolis 500 and their important place in Indiana's history and culture. Through an Indiana Academic Standards–based curriculum, the program offers a variety of interesting and thought-provoking lessons and projects and a unique opportunity to visit the Indianapolis Motor Speedway for an educational study trip during the months of April and May.

Indiana Academic Standards–based lesson plans are designed to give students an appreciation of the events and history of the 500 Festival and Indianapolis Motor Speedway. Lesson plans are free to schools enrolled in the program.

THE 500 FESTIVAL PRINCESS PROGRAM

The 500 Festival Princess Program celebrates Indiana's most civic-minded, poised, and academically driven young women. Each year, thirty-three college-aged women are selected as 500 Festival Princesses and serve as ambassadors of the 500 Festival, their hometowns, and their colleges/universities. Serving as a 500 Festival Princess provides young women with once-in-a-lifetime experiences as well as opportunities for leadership and professional development. Since the program's founding in 1959, more than eighteen hundred Indiana women have experienced the honor of being selected as a 500 Festival Princess.[2]

The 500 Festival princesses.

Miss Congeniality 2009 Jenna Liechty.

THE 500 FESTIVAL KIDSFIT PROGRAM

In an effort to fight childhood obesity, the KidsFit Program encourages Indiana youth to be more active and pursue a healthy lifestyle. This fitness program helps spark interest in walking and running and encourages fitness-related activities among Indiana youth and families. These ten- and twelve-week free, in-class curriculums target grades K–6 across the state of Indiana. Participants of the program complete weekly step-by-step lessons/activities with an Indianapolis 500 theme. In addition to the weekly curriculum activities, students are expected to complete one mile running or walking throughout each week leading up to the OneAmerica 500 Festival Mini-Marathon. The goal is for students to run 13.1 miles over the course of the program, the equivalent of a half marathon.

THE 500 FESTIVAL VOLUNTEER PROGRAM, PRESENTED BY CITIZENS ENERGY

More than seven thousand volunteers lend a hand throughout the month of May to help execute all of the 500 Festival events.

The volunteer program provides great opportunities for groups, organizations, and companies to engage in team building while supporting the community.

THE 500 FESTIVAL CORPORATE MEMBER PROGRAM

Composed of more than two hundred companies, the Corporate Member Program unites businesses around the 500 Festival's mission: to enrich lives, celebrate the Indianapolis 500, and foster positive impact on the city of Indianapolis and state of Indiana. Membership offers opportunities to build and maintain meaningful connections and increase companies' visibility.

THE 500 INTERNSHIP PROGRAM

The 500 Festival Internship Program offers opportunities for undergraduate students to gain valuable, real-world experience. Each year, college students from across the United States gain beneficial professional experience and a behind-the-scenes view of one of the nation's largest and most diverse festivals. Festival internships are only offered during the spring semester of the academic year.[3]

22

THE COKE LOT

OFFICIALLY DESIGNATED LOT 1C, THE "COKE LOT" IS LOCATED OUTSIDE Turn 4 at the intersection of Georgetown Road and West 25th Street. So nicknamed because it is adjacent to the Coca-Cola Bottling Plant, the site has been long known for its revelry and all-night partying, especially the night before the race. Typically the lot opens a few days before the race and is a festive site for motorhomes, campers, and tent campers.

While the "Coke Lot" is the best known, several other camp sites are situated in the vicinity of the track. Some provide family-friendly environments, while others cater to high-end motorhomes.[1]

Lot 1C—"Coke Lot."

23

THE SNAKE PIT

ORIGINALLY LOCATED IN THE INFIELD INSIDE TURN 1, THE SNAKE PIT was an area populated primarily by college-age fans seeking the ultimate party experience. For many it was considered a rite of spring. This was an area of extreme rowdiness, and it provided an opportunity to party with abandon.

In the 1980s bleachers were constructed in the area, along with a parking lot for competitor motorhomes, and improvements were made to Gasoline Alley, and other support buildings, effectively limiting the size of the Snake Pit. As a result, the fans migrated to the infield inside Turn 4, and a less intense Snake Pit 2 emerged.

Due largely to increased law enforcement presence, the level of extreme revelry dropped drastically in the 1990s to the point where the Snake Pit became more of a festive zone.

In 1999 the infield inside Turn 4 was razed to accommodate the new road course, virtually eliminating Snake Pit 2. This time the party crowd migrated to the infield inside Turn 3. By 2010 management embraced the area and officially named it the New Snake Pit. To entertain the crowd in a more controlled and festive environment, a concert stage is erected for race day, and popular bands and disc jockeys perform to the delight of all in attendance.[1]

Welcome to the Snake Pit!

24

ARMED FORCES DAY

THE INDIANAPOLIS MOTOR SPEEDWAY HAS CONDUCTED ACTIVITIES honoring the US military and Armed Forces Day since 1978. Armed Forces Day was created in 1949 to replace the separate Army, Navy, and Air Force Days and was first celebrated May 20, 1950, and is celebrated annually on the third Saturday of May.[1]

These activities have included military equipment displays, presentation of colors, ceremonial remarks, a musical presentation by a military band, and an oath of enlistment for those who have chosen to represent and defend our country.

On March 7, 2006, the Indianapolis Motor Speedway was honored with an award signifying its participation as a member of America Supports You, a Defense Department initiative to facilitate grassroots and corporate support for America's troops and their families.[2]

At the award presentation, Deputy Assistant Secretary of Defense for Public Affairs at the US Navy Memorial Allison Barber said, "I'm here on behalf of the Secretary of Defense to present the Indianapolis Motor Speedway with an award that signifies the importance of when corporations and communities reach out and support our military members and their families. We're thrilled to be here tonight to highlight the long tradition of the Indianapolis Motor Speedway and their support for our military."[3]

Upon accepting the Office of the Secretary of Defense Medal for Exceptional Public Service, Joie Chitwood, then president and chief operating officer of Indianapolis Motor Speedway, said, "On behalf of

America's heroes.

the (speedway's owners), it's an honor to be here tonight and to accept this recognition. "We have a unique event that is specifically tied in to Memorial Day weekend.... It only makes the greatest spectacle in racing that much more special."[4]

25

RADIO AND "THE GREATEST SPECTACLE IN RACING"

IN THE MID-1920S, RADIO BROADCASTS OF THE 500 WERE LITTLE MORE than a few minutes of coverage of the start and finish, with updates every fifteen or thirty minutes in between. In 1952 the speedway created its own network and followed the same format.

In 1953 the race was covered in its entirety from start to finish. The only breaks were those for commercials. As the number of subscribing stations skyrocketed, station representatives were solicited for comment and feedback. The most common response was a request for a method to alert station engineers of impending commercial breaks using a standard out-cue.

The sales staff of radio station WIBC of Indianapolis, the network's flagship station, was tasked with finding an answer to the request. A female copywriter in her early twenties named Alice Greene suggested a phrase destined to become the best-known and most-beloved moniker of any sporting event in the world.

In 1954 for the first time the world heard Sid Collins, chief announcer for the Indianapolis Motor Speedway Network, speak the enduring phrase, "Stay tuned for the Greatest Spectacle in Racing."

Before ABC first carried the Indianapolis 500-Mile Race live and in its entirety on television in 1986, radio was the only source of live coverage of the race. Millions of fans who could not be in attendance would sit glued to their radios whether they were at home, enjoying Memorial Day family picnics, or simply sitting in their cars. Those who lived during those days look back on them fondly and can remember many of the race calls verbatim. Announcers expertly painted pictures that to this day still live in the minds of those fortunate to experience them. It truly was a golden age in radio broadcast history.

Since 1971 and continuing to this day, the most popular daily radio show during the month of May has been Donald Davidson's "The Talk of Gasoline Alley."[1] Davidson delves into the past and the present as he entertains questions and comments solicited through telephone calls and social media.

Sid Collins in 1960 at the microphone.

26

THE GORDON PIPERS

SINCE 1963 THE GORDON PIPERS, A SCOTTISH/CELTIC BAGPIPE BAND, have been a fixture during Indianapolis 500 ceremonies, including opening day, qualifications, the 500 Festival Parade, and race day.[1] Tony Hulman, owner of the Indianapolis Motor Speedway, first heard a performance by the Pipers in June 1962 at the Hoosier Grand Prix, their first notable performance. Duly impressed, he invited the group to perform at the 1963 Indianapolis 500 as the "Gasoline Alley Gordon Pipers."

Each year four bagpipers greet the winner in Victory Lane for the drink of milk and the Borg-Warner Trophy presentation. These four pipers signify the winning car arriving in Victory Lane on four wheels safely.

The bagpipe band was founded early in 1962. Wallace Gordon Diehl, John Hudgins, Bill Cochran, and Bill Simpson—members of the Murat Highlanders Bagpipe Band—conceived the idea of an unrestricted bagpipe band. The name Gordon Pipers was chosen to honor Diehl, and it was decided the pipers would wear the dress Gordon tartan while the drummers would be dressed in the Wallace tartan.[2]

The Gordon Pipers make their way down the front stretch.

PART 3

RACE DAY

Race day at Indianapolis is unlike any other day in sports. For the fans it is a day that has been 364 days in the waiting. For the officials it is a day that has been planned years in advance. For the drivers and teams, it is the culmination of a lifetime of dreams.

The Indianapolis 500-Mile Race is the world's largest, single-day sporting event. Hundreds of thousands of spectators are in attendance. Many occupy the quarter-million reserved seats that have been held by families for generations. Others seek their favorite spots on the infield viewing mounds. There are no bad seats at Indianapolis. If you are fortunate enough to attend the Indianapolis 500, you have a good seat.

The prerace festivities are filled with pageantry and ceremony as the anticipation of the start of the great race builds to a pinnacle of emotion rarely experienced by sports fans. The morning program is a series of carefully scripted events and has changed little over the years.

Shown below is the schedule for The 100th Running of the Indianapolis 500.[1]

Previous page, It's race day!

6:00 A.M. Public gates open

7:00 A.M. Snake Pit presented by Coors Light opens

8:00 A.M. Spectacle of Bands

8:00 A.M. Borg-Warner Trophy march to the Bricks

9:45 A.M. 500 Festival Princess lap

10:15 A.M. "On the Banks of the Wabash" performed by the
Purdue University All-American Marching Band

10:15 A.M. Cars grid on track

10:35 A.M. Green flag delivered in Turn 1 by IU Health Helicopter

10:50 A.M. Vintage race car laps

11:10 A.M. Military recognition lap

11:37 A.M. Driver introductions

11:54 P.M. "America the Beautiful"

11:56 A.M. Military address

12:00 P.M. Invocation

12:01 P.M. "Taps"

12:02 P.M. "God Bless America"

12:05 P.M. National anthem

12:06 P.M. Flyover

12:06 P.M. "Drivers to your cars" announcement

12:16 P.M. "Back Home Again in Indiana" and Balloon Spectacle

12:17 P.M. "Lady and Gentlemen, Start Your Engines"

12:20 P.M. VERIZON INDYCAR SERIES | Race
100th Running of the Indianapolis 500 presented by PennGrade
Motor Oil (200 laps)

6:00 P.M. Public gates close

And the day literally starts with a *bang!*

27

PERCUSSION GRENADES

·

BANG! IT'S RACE DAY AT INDIANAPOLIS! TYPICALLY TWO PERCUSSION grenades or aerial military bombs are fired in the morning to signify the speedway gates are now open. This usually occurs at 6:00 a.m.; however, some years it is earlier based on the television broadcast schedule.

It is believed this practice has been followed since the very first race as a way to notify security it is time to open the gates to this enormous facility.

The percussions can be heard for miles around, and it is a most welcome sound to all who will be in attendance.

28

SPECTACLE OF BANDS

THE FIRST OFFICIAL EVENT OF PRE-RACE FESTIVITIES IS THE Spectacle of Bands. Typically beginning at 8:00 a.m., this long and storied tradition dates back several decades.

The Purdue University Department of Bands and Orchestras produces this event, which over the years has included musicians from various communities, fraternal organizations, industries, schools, universities, and the military. Patriotic and pop songs are played as the bands march around the famed two-and-a-half mile oval.

Over the years more than 180,000 musicians have taken approximately 970 million steps in front of thousands of early risers.[1] Some fans make it to their seats hours before the race to enjoy the spectacle while others will take to the track at the end of the front straightaway and line the outside wall to witness the processional up close.

To date, Johnny Parsons, the son of 1950 Indianapolis 500 winner Johnnie Parsons, is the only person to participate in the Spectacle of Bands both as a musician and later in life as a driver in the race. He played trumpet for the Scecina High School Marching Band in Indianapolis, and from 1974 to 1996 he drove in twelve Indianapolis 500 races. "My sister Joan was the head majorette and I marched in my sophomore and junior years in 1961 and 1962, and it was really cool to do that on the track that our father won on and where I had watched so many races there," said Parsons, whose father Johnnie won the race in 1950.[2]

The annual Spectacle of Bands is the perfect start to the greatest day in motorsport.

High school bands from across the country have participated in this race day tradition since 1922.

29

THE 500 FESTIVAL PRINCESSES

SINCE THE PROGRAM'S FOUNDING IN 1959, MORE THAN 1,800 INDIANA women have experienced the honor of being selected as a 500 Festival Princess.

The 500 Festival Princess Program celebrates Indiana's most civic-minded and academically driven young women. Each year, 33 college-aged women are selected as 500 Festival Princesses and serve as ambassadors of the 500 Festival, participating in outreach in their hometowns, at their colleges/universities, and in Indianapolis.[1] They are chosen from hundreds of applicants based on communication skills, academic performance, and community involvement.

Each young woman in the 500 Festival Princess program receives a $1,000 scholarship and participates in the 500 Festival Leadership Development Program, encouraging and empowering the women to make an impact in their communities and in the state of Indiana. Serving as a 500 Festival Princess provides young women with once-in-a-life-time experiences and countless opportunities for personal and professional development.

The 500 Festival Princesses attend and volunteer at all 500 Festival events during the month of May as well as prerace festivities and Victory Circle celebrations. The prerace festivities include a ceremonial lap around the track by the 500 Festival queen and her court. Chauffeured in hospitality vehicles, the queen and each member of her court make their way around the famed oval to the delight of thousands of fans. For each, it is an experience unlike any other, and it is one not likely to be forgotten.

An unforgettable lap around the track.

THE INDIANAPOLIS 500

30

PURDUE UNIVERSITY ALL-AMERICAN MARCHING BAND

THE PURDUE UNIVERSITY ALL-AMERICAN MARCHING BAND HAS BEEN the host band of the Indianapolis 500 since 1919. Located in West Lafayette, Indiana, the band was founded in 1886 when students of the Army Training Corps formed a five-member drum corps, accompanying cadets during morning conditioning marches. The band has grown to nearly four hundred members today.[1]

Paul Spotts Emrick, the band's first director, was the one responsible for developing the relationship with the Indianapolis 500 in 1919. In 2019 the band will be making its hundredth appearance as it participates in opening ceremonies as it accompanies guest vocalists and performs pop tunes and patriotic and ceremonial music. The band has participated annually in the 500 Festival Parade since its inception in 1957.[2]

Two of the more recognizable symbols of the band are the World's Largest Drum and the Golden Girl. The drum rises to a height of more than ten feet as it sits on its carriage. It was commissioned by Director Emrick in 1921 and constructed by the Leedy Manufacturing Company of Indianapolis. It has been part of the tradition and history of the Indianapolis 500 ever since.[3]

In 1954 band director Al G. Wright convinced one of the nation's great baton twirlers, Juanita Carpenter of Colorado, to attend Purdue University with the idea of putting her in front of the band. At the top of her art form and blessed with a terrific personality, Carpenter would be perfect for the role of ambassador for the university and the band. During that era Len Dawson was quarterback for the Purdue football team. His poise

The Golden Girl and the Purdue University All-American Marching Band.

and accomplishments soon earned him the nickname "Golden Boy." It only seemed fitting Carpenter would be known as the "Golden Girl."

From Juanita Carpenter to the 2017–2018 Golden Girl Kaitlyn Schleis there have been thirty Golden Girls who have served as leaders of the All-American Marching Band and as ambassadors of Purdue University.[4]

31

CELEBRITY GUESTS

CELEBRITIES HAVE LONG BEEN PRESENT AT THE INDIANAPOLIS 500. Television and movie stars, recording artists, sports figures, members of the military, and politicians are among the invited guests. The parade of stars around the track during prerace festivities is a fan favorite.

Guests including Mike Pence, Jim Nabors, James Garner, Dan Quayle, David Letterman, Tim Allen, Florence Henderson, Jay Leno, and Linda Vaughn have attended multiple years. Additionally, several NASA astronauts were among the invited guests during the 1960s and 1970s.

Paul Newman attended the race many times. From 1983 to 1995 and again in 2008, he was at the race as co-owner of Newman-Haas Racing.

Clark Gable can be seen in a famous picture from the 1947 race sitting with track owner Tony Hulman in Turn 1. The photograph hangs in the Indianapolis Motor Speedway Museum on the grounds of the Indianapolis Motor Speedway.[1]

Former presidents Gerald Ford, George H. W. Bush, and Bill Clinton have also attended the race. You never know whom you might see within the confines of the Indianapolis Motor Speedway.

Tony Hulman with Clark Gable in 1947.

32

"ON THE BANKS OF THE WABASH"

AS PART OF THE SPECTACLE OF BANDS, THE PURDUE UNIVERSITY All-American Marching Band plays several songs, including "On the Banks of the Wabash," as they parade around the track. Written and composed by Indiana native Paul Dresser, it was published in October 1897. On March 14, 1913, the Indiana General Assembly adopted the song as the official state song.

"On the Banks of the Wabash, Far Away"
Round my Indiana homestead wave the cornfields,
In the distance loom the woodlands clear and cool.
Oftentimes my thoughts revert to scenes of childhood,
Where I first received my lessons, nature's school.
But one thing there is missing from the picture,
Without her face it seems so incomplete
I long to see my mother in the doorway,
As she stood there years ago, her boy to greet.

(Chorus)

Oh, the moonlight's fair tonight along the Wabash,
From the fields there comes the breath of newmown hay.
Through the sycamores the candle lights are gleaming.

On the banks of the Wabash, far away.

(Verse)

Many years have passed since I strolled by the river,
Arm in arm, with sweetheart Mary by my side,

It was there I tried to tell her that I loved her,
It was there I begged of her to be my bride.
Long years have passed since I strolled thro' the churchyard.
She's sleeping there, my angel, Mary dear,
I loved her but she thought I didn't mean it,
Still I'd give my future were she only here.[1]

33

"AMERICA THE BEAUTIFUL" AND "GOD BLESS AMERICA"

FROM 1991 UNTIL THE YEAR BEFORE SHE PASSED IN LATE 2016, Florence Henderson performed "America the Beautiful" or "God Bless America" most years. A friend of the Hulman-George family and a native Hoosier, Henderson first performed "America the Beautiful" in 1991 during the prerace festivities leading to the seventy-fifth running of the Indianapolis 500-Mile Race. She repeated her performance in 1992, but from 1993 to 1997, she switched to the national anthem before returning to "America the Beautiful" from 1999 to 2002.

From 2003 through 2015, Henderson performed "God Bless America" as more than three hundred thousand fans joined her in song. It is truly something to experience as the words reverberate through the man-made canyon that is the front stretch.

In 2016 the Indianapolis Children's Choir performed "God Bless America." Henderson served as the Grand Marshall for the hundredth running of the Indianapolis 500-Mile Race.

In 2017 the 101st Airborne Division Band accompanied vocalist Rick Walburn as he sang "America the Beautiful," and in 2018 the song was performed by the Indiana National Guard Trio accompanied by the Purdue All-American Band.

"God Bless America" was sung by Angela Brown in 2017 and by Jon McLaughlin in 2018.[1]

Florence Henderson.

34

NATIONAL ANTHEM

MOST YEARS THE "STAR-SPANGLED BANNER" IS PRESENTED PRIOR TO the race. Through the early 1980s, the national anthem was typically performed by the Purdue University All-American Band without a vocalist. In 1970 Al Hirt offered a trumpet solo, and in 1976, to honor the bicentennial, Tom Sullivan and Up with People were invited to sing.

Notable artists have been asked to sing the national anthem, accompanied by the Purdue Band, throughout the years, beginning in the mid-1980s. These artists have included James Hubert, Robert McFarlin, David Hasselhoff, Sandi Patti, and Florence Henderson (both Patti and Henderson on numerous occasions), Major Lisa Kopczynski, LeAnn Rimes, and members of the US Armed Forces.

In 2015 former *American Idol* winner and recording artist Jordin Sparks honored America with her rendition of the "Star-Spangled Banner."

Singer and songwriter Darius Rucker, founder of the Grammy Award–winning group Hootie and the Blowfish, performed the national anthem in 2016.

Singer/songwriter Bebe Rexha honored America in 2017, and multiple Grammy Award winning-superstar Kelly Clarkson performed in 2018.[1]

The Stars and Stripes on the front stretch.

35

FLYOVER

IN MOST YEARS SINCE 1991, A MILITARY FLYOVER HAS FOLLOWED the conclusion of the national anthem. The "missing man formation" has been executed some years when multiple aircraft are involved. In 2011 there was a postrace flyover with four F/A-18E Superhornets to honor the hundredth anniversary of the inaugural Indianapolis 500-Mile Race.

1991: Four A-10s

1992: The "Black Aces"

1994: Four P-51 Mustangs, led by Chuck Yeager

1995: B-17 Flying Fortress, led by Chuck Yeager

1996: Four F-18 Hornets (Marine Aircraft Group 31)

1997: Stealth Bomber

1999: Stealth Bomber & four F-14 Tomcats

2000: Two AV-8B Harrier IIs

2001: Four F-16s, "The Racers" (181st Fighter Wing, Indiana Air National Guard)

2002: Stealth Bomber "Spirit of Washington" (509th Bomb Wing, Whiteman Air Force Base)

2003: Stealth Bomber "Spirit of Indiana" (509th Bomb Wing, Whiteman Air Force Base)

2004: Four F-16s, "The Black Snakes" (122d Fighter Wing, Air National Guard)

2005: Stealth Bomber

2006: Historic Aircraft & four F-16s

2007: Four F-22 Raptors (Langley AFB)

2008: Two F-16 Vipers & two F/A-18 Hornets (Naval Strike and Air Warfare Center)

2009: Two WWII B-25 Mitchell bombers

2010: Four F/A-18 Hornets (Naval Strike and Air Warfare Center)

2011: Prerace: Stealth Bomber "Spirit of Indiana" (509th Bomb Wing, Whiteman Air Force Base); Postrace: Four F/A-18E Superhornets

2012: A-10 Thunderbolt "Warthog," F-16 Fighting Falcon, two P-51 Mustangs

2013: One WWII North American B-25 Mitchell (Tri-State Warbird Museum) and five North American T-6 Texan trainer aircraft

2014: Black Diamond Jet Team

2015: Two A-10 Warthogs from the Indiana Air National Guard.

2016: Douglas SBD-5 Dauntless and P-51 Mustang in collaboration with the Commemorative Air Force and two F/A-18E Superhornets from VFA-81 flying in formation with two EA-18G Growlers from VAQ-139

2017: B-52 Bomber (69th Bomb Squadron)

2018: B-52 Stealth Bomber from Whiteman AFB[1]

Stealth Bomber in 2011.

36

INVOCATION

THE INDIANAPOLIS 500-MILE RACE WAS MOVED TO THE SUNDAY OF Memorial Day weekend beginning in 1974, at which time an invocation was added to the prerace ceremonies. Most years a representative of the Roman Catholic Archdiocese of Indianapolis has been invited to deliver the prayer. Occasionally famous clergymen have been asked to do the honor, including Oral Roberts in 1977 and Billy Graham in 1999.[1]

From 1993 to 2009, Archbishop Daniel M. Buechlein delivered the invocation with the exceptions of 1997, 1999, and 2004. He would typically end his prayer with the word "Godspeed" in the languages of all of the drivers in the starting field.

In 2015 and 2016, the invocation was delivered by Archbishop Joseph William Tobin.[2]

Father Michael Welch delivered the invocation in 2017, and in 2018 Archbishop Charles C. Thompson gave the prayer.[3]

Pastor Billy Graham in 1999.

37

REMARKS

BEGINNING IN 2000, A MILITARY OR GOVERNMENT OFFICIAL HAS offered remarks as part of the prerace ceremonies. In 2009 a three-volley salute was added at the conclusion of the remarks.

2000: US Secretary of Defense William Cohen

2001: General James L. Jones

2003: General Jack Keane

2004: General William J. Begert

2005: General Colin Powell (former US Secretary of State)

2006: General Colin Powell (former US Secretary of State)

2007: General Norman Schwarzkopf Jr.

2008: General Victor E. Renuart Jr.

2009: General Craig R. McKinley, followed by a three-volley salute

2010: Rear Admiral John W. Miller, followed by a three-volley salute

2011: General Peter W. Chiarelli, followed by a three-volley salute

2012: Admiral James A. Winnefeld Jr., followed by a three-volley salute

2013: Colonel Jack H. Jacobs, followed by a three-volley salute

2014: General Frank J. Grass, followed by a three-volley salute

2015: General Dennis L. Via, followed by a three-volley salute

2016: Lieutenant General Joseph Anderson and a tribute to Pearl Harbor survivors, followed by a three-volley salute

2017: General Robert B. Abrams, followed by a three-volley salute

2018: General Joseph L. Lengyel, followed by a three-volley salute

Honoring Pearl Harbor survivors in 2016.

For the past several years a preamble honoring those who have fallen in combat and those who have lost their lives in auto racing has been recited by a member of the Indianapolis Motor Speedway public address announcing team:[1]

The Preamble

On this Memorial Day Weekend, we pause in a moment of silence, to pay homage to those individuals who have given their lives—unselfishly, and unafraid—so that we may witness as free men and women, the world's greatest sporting event.

We also pay homage to those individuals, who have given their lives—unselfishly and without fear—to make racing the world's most spectacular spectator sport.

38

"TAPS"

OF ALL THE PRERACE FESTIVITIES, NONE IS HELD IN HIGHER ESTEEM than the playing of "Taps" to honor those men and women who have given their lives in defense of our freedoms and our nation. More than three hundred thousand fans stand in absolute silence as the tribute is rendered, and they remain so for several moments following.

A combined US Armed Forces Color Guard performed the song in the 1960s and 1970s. From 1980 to 2005, the Purdue University All-American Marching Band had the honor on several occasions.

Since 2006, a trumpet solo by a member of the US Armed Forces has been performed.

1980:	Purdue University Brass Quartet
1983–1984:	Purdue University All-American Marching Band
1985:	Combined US Armed Forces Color Guard
1986:	Ron Blomberg and Robert A. Nixon (74th Army Band of Fort Benjamin Harrison)
1987–1996:	Purdue University All-American Marching Band
1997:	Larry Wiseman
1998–2005:	Purdue University All-American Marching Band
2006–2008:	Sgt. Byron Bartosh (Indiana National Guard)
2009–2010:	Sgt. Joseph Young (Indiana National Guard)
2011–2018:	SSG Ron Duncan[1]

39

"BACK HOME AGAIN IN INDIANA"

THE SINGING OF "BACK HOME AGAIN IN INDIANA" DURING PRERACE festivities is one of the more enduring traditions of the Indianapolis 500. Originally titled "Indiana" and released in 1917, the song was written by James F. Hanley and Ballard MacDonald.

There are reports that "Back Home Again in Indiana" was played by a brass band in 1919 as Howdy Wilcox drove his closing laps on his way to victory, but it wasn't until 1946 that the song became a regular part of the 500's festivities. New York Metropolitan Opera Company member James Melton was an avid collector of antique cars as well as president of the Antique Automobile Club of America at one time. He provided several vehicles that took part in the prerace festivities in 1946. Prior to the race he performed the song with the Purdue University "All-American" Marching Band. It was so well received he was invited back the following year. In 1948 the singing was scheduled to occur just prior to the command to start engines. It remains in that time slot to this day.

Through the years performers have included Mel Tormé, Vic Damone, Dinah Shore, Ed Ames, Peter Marshall, Dennis Morgan, and Johnny Desmond. Jim Nabors performed the song from 1972 to 2014, missing only a handful of years.[1]

Citing health reasons, Nabors sang at the speedway for the final time in 2014. He has been followed by the Indiana-based a cappella group Straight No Chaser in 2015 and Indianapolis resident and winner of NBC'S *The Voice* Josh Kaufman in 2016. Since 2017, professional singer James Cornelison, who performs "The Star Bangled Banner" for the Chicago Blackhawks hockey team, and "O Canada" when they are

Jim Nabors in 2014.

hosting a Canadian team, has thrilled fans with his rendition of this fan favorite.

"BACK HOME AGAIN IN INDIANA" CHORUS

Back home again in Indiana,
   And it seems that I can see
The gleaming candlelight, still shining bright,
   Through the sycamores for me.
The new-mown hay sends all its fragrance
   From the fields I used to roam.
When I dream about the moonlight on the Wabash,
   Then I long for my Indiana home.[2]

40

BALLOON SPECTACLE

GRACE SMITH HULMAN, TONY HULMAN'S MOTHER, SUGGESTED multicolored, helium-filled balloons be released the morning of the race to further the day's excitement. In 1947 the first launch occurred. Since 1950 the liftoff has coincided with the closing notes of the playing of "Back Home Again in Indiana" as thousands of balloons grace the Indiana heavens. They can often be seen in the distant sky during the early laps of the race.

This is perhaps the most exciting time for millions of fans around the world who have waited a year in eager anticipation for that which is next on the program, the command to start engines!

Up, up, and away!

41

THE COMMAND

THE CALL TO START ENGINES IS MADE BY SIMPLY STATING: "Gentlemen, start your engines!" If there are female drivers in the field, the call is amended to, "Lady and gentlemen . . ." or "Ladies and gentlemen . . ."

There are conflicting accounts as to the origin of the phrase, the first to recite it, and the exact wording of it.[1] Prior to World War II, an aerial bomb would signal the start of engines.[2]

The first verified recitation was by public address announcer John Francis "Irish" Horan in 1950.[3] Some reports claim Seth Klein, chief starter for the race, gave the command the following year.[4] Some claim it was Horan.[5] Either Klein or Horan said it again in 1952.[6]

In the early 1950s, the command was changed from "motors" to "engines." Officials and participants favored the more technical term "engines" when describing their machines. Harlan Fengler, the chief steward, explained to radio announcer Sid Collins, "There are no motors in the race, just engines."[7]

There was a time when Wilbur Shaw, three-time Indianapolis 500 champion and president of the speedway from 1946 to 1954, was believed to be the one who coined the phrase. It was claimed in his autobiography he recited the command at all post–World War II races.[8] Donald Davidson, track historian, believes Shaw only recited it in 1953 and 1954.

Following Shaw's passing in October 1954, track owner Tony Hulman assumed the duty and honor of giving the command. Hulman was normally a shy and soft-spoken individual, but when it came time to pronounce those most famous four words, he exhibited a proud and vociferous voice, raising a clinched fist and turning it much as one would turn an automobile ignition switch, stirring the hearts of all who heard him.

Following Tony Human's passing in 1977, either his widow, Mary F. Hulman, or his daughter, Mari Hulman-George, has done the honor.

Janet Guthrie became the first woman to qualify for the Indianapolis 500 in 1977, and controversy soon arose regarding the command, "Gentlemen, start your engines!" Management did not want to amend the traditional phrase.[9] Cars were actually started by male crew members with electric handheld starters at the rear of the cars. Displeased by the position taken by management, especially in light of Guthrie's unprecedented accomplishment, the crew responded by assigning Kay Bignotti, the wife of mechanic George Bignotti, as the crew member responsible for operating the inertial starter at the rear of Guthrie's car.

In light of this new development, the speedway opted for a special command for that year, but it was not announced in advance.[10] On May 29, 1977, Tony Hulman spoke the highly anticipated phrase: "In company with the first lady ever to qualify at Indianapolis, gentlemen, start your engines!" After Guthrie qualified again in 1978 and 1979, the command was amended to "Lady and gentlemen, start your engines!"

Lyn St. James became the second woman to ever qualify for the race in 1992. Her request to change the command to "Drivers, start your engines!" was dismissed, and the command used was the now customary, "Lady and gentlemen, start your engines!" or "Ladies and gentlemen, start your engines!" if there are two or more women in the field.

Most times the command was given in front of the starting grid at the pace car. Jim Philippe, the public address announcer, would introduce the command with the words "traditional command" or the "famous four words." His final Indianapolis 500 was 2003. For many years through 1989, Luke Walton would introduce the command on the radio network broadcast. Dave Calabro has introduced the command since 2004 by calling it the "most famous words in motorsports."

Most often Tony Hulman would ride in the pace car during the pace laps following the command.

In time the command location was moved near the start/finish line. In 2001 it was again moved to the new victory podium stage adjacent the pagoda. In celebration of the hundredth anniversary of the inaugural Indianapolis 500-Mile Race in 2011, Mari Hulman-George moved back to the front of the starting grid to give the command and rode in the pace car driven by four-time Indianapolis 500 champion A. J. Foyt.

In 2014, for the first time since 1954, a nonmember of the Hulman-George family gave the command. To honor Jim Nabors's final performance of "Back Home Again in Indiana," he and Mari Hulman-George gave the command in unison.

On those occasions when the race has been halted due to rain or an accident, a second command has been given once it is time to resume the race. That command is: "Restart your engines!"[11]

For the hundredth running of the Indianapolis 500 in 2016, four generations of the Hulman-George family recited the command in unison from atop the victory podium.

Tony Hulman in 1969. "Gentlemen, start your engines!"

Above, Mrs. Hulman-George in 2015. "Ladies and gentlemen, start your engines!"

Below, Four generations of the Hulman-George family give the command to start engines for the 100th Running of the Indianapolis 500-Mile Race in 2016.

42

PACE CAR

THE INAUGURAL RUNNING OF THE INDIANAPOLIS 500-MILE RACE IN 1911 saw forty cars meeting qualification requirements. Track founder Carl Fisher is credited with the concept of a "flying start" or "rolling start" as opposed to the common practice of a "standing start" used at nearly all races at that time. Prior to the start of the inaugural Indianapolis 500 in 1911, Fisher believed it would be safer to lead the field on one unscored lap with a pace car at approximately 40–45 mph and then release the field to the starter as the pace car pulled into the pits. This practice has been employed at every Indianapolis 500 and is used extensively at many tracks and at many races around the world today.

From 1911 to 1956, the pace car led the field to the green flag on one unscored lap at a predetermined speed. This one lap would be used to warm up the engines and the tires. The first pace car was a 1911 Stoddard-Dayton. Through the years, many manufacturers have supplied the pace car for the race, including General Motors, Fiat, Ford, Dodge, Studebaker, Stoddard Dayton, and Stutz.

Carl Fisher drove the first pace car in 1911 and continued to do so through 1915. Over the years it has been deemed a privilege and an honor to be selected to lead the field to the green flag. Former winners of the 500, such as Sam Hanks, Rodger Ward, Wilbur Shaw, Jim Rathmann, Bobby Unser, Parnelli Jones, Emerson Fittipaldi, A. J. Foyt, and Dario Franchitti have all had the honor, as well as celebrities including Jay Leno, Morgan Freeman, Patrick Dempsey, Lance Armstrong, General Colin Powell, Jim Caviezel, Carroll Shelby, Chuck Yeager, Edsel Ford, Guy Fieri, and former track owner Captain Eddie Rickenbacker.

Tommy Milton, the first two-time winner of the 500 (1921 and 1923), was asked to drive the pace car for the 1936 race. He accepted the invitation based on the condition the pace car be awarded to the winner of the race. Officials agreed, and Louis Meyer was presented a brand-new 1936 Packard 120 for his victory. This practice has been continued every year since.

In 1957 the practice was extended to include the pace car leading the field for two laps before the green flag. This was very popular, as it gave the drivers an opportunity to salute the fans and provided opportunities for spectacular photographs of the rolling field. It also allowed the drivers the opportunity to further survey track conditions as they warmed up their engines and tires. The two-lap format remained in place through 1976.[1]

In 1977 the format was modified and included two parade laps and one pace lap, and it has been in place ever since. This practice has provided the drivers even more time for warm-up before forming the field in eleven distinct rows of three for the start of the race.[2]

Through 1978, the pace car was used only at the start of the race. Starting in 1979, the pace car has also been used during caution periods to pick up the leader and pack up the field at a reduced speed. The ceremonial driver drives only at the start of the race. During caution periods a trained official is the driver.[3]

In 2015 Jeff Gordon, four-time NASCAR Series champion and former resident of Indiana, piloted the pace car at the start of the race. Once the race began, full-time Verizon IndyCar Series pace car driver Johnny Rutherford (three-time Indianapolis 500 champion) drove the pace car for the remainder of the race. In 2016 Rutherford retired, and Sarah Fisher (longtime driver and car owner) assumed the position as full-time pace car driver.

A list of pace cars and drivers through the years can be found in the appendix.

Above, Roger Penske brings the field to the green flag in 2016.

Below, Fiftieth anniversary Chevrolet Camaro SS set to pace the field for the 100th Running of the Indianapolis 500-Mile Race.

43

HONORARY STARTER

A RELATIVELY NEW TRADITION OF THE 500 IS THAT OF A SPECIAL guest invited to serve as an honorary starter. In 1993 Nick Fornoro, former CART starter who retired in 1992, was the first to receive this honor. The guests who have followed him have been from industry, entertainment, sports, government, and the military.

The tradition was expanded in 2013 to include an additional celebrity in accompaniment with a patient or patients from nearby Riley Children's Hospital. Arriving by helicopter, they ceremoniously deliver the green flag to the honorary starter.[1]

> 1993: Nick Fornoro (retired CART starter, retired at the end of the 1992 CART season)
>
> 1996: Robert James Eaton (chairman and CEO of Chrysler Corporation)
>
> 1997: General Ronald Fogleman (chief of staff of the US Air Force)
>
> 1998: Mark Page (senior vice president of store operations for Pep Boys, IndyCar Series sponsor)
>
> 1999: Jim Postl (president and CEO of Pennzoil)
>
> 2000: Howard Katz (president of ABC Sports)
>
> 2004: Nick Lachey (entertainer)
>
> 2005: Reggie Miller (former player for the Indiana Pacers)
>
> 2006: Sugar Ray Leonard (professional boxer)

2007: Peyton Manning (former quarterback for the Indianapolis Colts)

2008: Kristi Yamaguchi (US Olympic figure skater)

2009: Allen Sirkin (COO of Phillips-Van Heusen, IndyCar Series sponsor)

2010: Jack Nicholson (actor)

2011: Bruce P. Crandall (Medal of Honor recipient)

2012: Mitch Daniels (Indiana governor)

2013: Michael Peña (actor, promoting the film *Turbo*)
- Green flag delivered by Chuck Pagano (former Indianapolis Colts head coach) and Riley Hospital patient Willie Avil

2014: Mark Cuban (Owner of NBA Dallas Mavericks and Entrepreneur)
- Green flag delivered by Andrew Luck (Indianapolis Colts quarterback) and Riley Hospital patients MaKenzi Rooksberry and Johliel Austin

2015: Patrick Dempsey (actor)
- Green flag delivered by Paul George (former Indiana Pacers player), Riley Hospital patient Tori Gwyn, and Pat McAfee (former Indianapolis Colts player)

2016: Chris Pine (actor)
- Green flag delivered by representatives of Indiana University Health

2017: Jake Gyllenhall (actor) and Jeff Bauman (Boston Marathon bombing survivor)
- Green flag delivered by Nathan Kress (actor) and workers from IU Health University Hospital

2018: Chris Hemsworth (actor)
- Green flag delivered by deadmau5 (producer, musician, and composer) after being transported by Governor Eric Holcomb via non-stop flight from Paris[2]

Jack Nicholson sends them on their way in 2010!

44

GREEN! GREEN! GREEN!

THE MOST THRILLING START TO ANY SPORTING EVENT IN THE WORLD is the start of the Indianapolis 500-Mile Race. After two and a half pace laps of saluting the crowd, warming tires and engines, making adjustments in the cockpit, and forming the field, the drivers and their machines are ready to go.

The pace car brings the field up to speed and then pulls off the race-course. Led by the pole sitter, thirty-three cars in eleven rows of three make their way out of Turn 4. The starter takes his or her position in the flag stand with green flag in hand.

More than three hundred thousand fans stand in anticipation. Their deafening thunder of approval is exceeded only by the sounds of the engines beckoning their masters to set them free as they make their way to the green flag. And then it happens!

Green! Green! Green!

Five hundred miles—two hundred laps, eight hundred turns—lie ahead. Lifetimes of dreams for thirty-three men and women are realized. They have started the Indianapolis 500, but there is much work to do. Years of hard work and millions of dollars have been spent for this moment, but there can be only one victor. Over the next three hours, there will be moments of victory and moments of defeat, but in the end, an Indianapolis 500 champion will be crowned, and a life will be changed forever.

Five hundred miles to go!

45

WINNERS DRINK MILK

POSSIBLY THE BEST-KNOWN INDIANAPOLIS 500 TRADITION IS THAT OF the winner drinking from a bottle of milk in Victory Lane immediately after the race. Like so many other traditions, it was not planned to become a custom, but circumstances and history destined it to become one of the great victory celebrations in all of sports.

Louis Meyer was raised in Los Angeles. On warm, summer days his mother would give him buttermilk to drink. She said it would give him renewed energy and revitalize him, and it was a practice Meyer followed regularly.

In 1936 Meyer won the Indianapolis 500-Mile Race. One of his crew members handed him a bottle of buttermilk while in Victory Lane, which he promptly drank.

The next morning an executive with the Milk Foundation saw the moment captured in a photograph in the sports section of his newspaper. Delighted, he vowed to ensure the practice would be repeated in coming years, and it was, through 1941. The race was suspended during World War II.

From 1947 to 1955, milk was not offered to the winner. The reason for this is unclear. The practice was renewed in 1956, and it has been repeated every year since with one exception.

Emerson Fittipaldi, the 1993 winner, owned citrus farms in his native Brazil. In an effort to promote his industry, he chose to drink orange juice instead of milk in Victory Lane. This was not well received by fans, management, or officials. At the urging of his car owner, Roger Penske, Fittipaldi finally relented and took a small sip of milk.

At the time of entry into the race, a driver is asked to select the type of milk he or she would prefer in Victory Lane. The choices are whole milk, one-percent milk, and skim milk. (If a driver were to be lactose intolerant, he or she could take only a very small sip and then pass the bottle around.)

Additionally, the milk cannot be flavored, such as chocolate or strawberry. The reason? Flavored milk does not photograph as well as plain, white milk.[1]

Dan Wheldon wins the 100th Anniversary Indianapolis 500-Mile Race!

46

KISSING THE BRICKS

IN 1996, NASCAR CHAMPION DALE JARRETT WON THE THIRD RUNNING of the Brickyard 400 for the NASCAR stock-car series at the famed oval. He and his crew chief, Todd Parrott, decided to walk to the start/finish line, kneel down, and literally kiss the Yard of Bricks to pay homage to the legendary history of the Indianapolis Motor Speedway. Soon after, the team joined them for a group kiss, and a tradition was born that continues to this day. When asked later how the bricks tasted, Dale Jarrett reportedly responded, "They tasted like victory."[1]

That tradition carried over to the Indianapolis 500 when winning driver Gil de Ferran and his crew kissed the bricks following their victory in 2003.[2]

The Indianapolis Motor Speedway Museum conducts grounds tours of the facility on a regular basis. The most popular stop for guests is the Yard of Bricks. Every year thousands of visitors, ranging in age from one to ninety-nine, follow Dale Jarrett's lead and kiss the bricks, leaving with memories and photographs they will cherish forever.

Alexander Rossi and team celebrate winning the hundredth running
of the Indianapolis 500-Mile Race.

47

THE BORG-WARNER TROPHY

IN 1935, BORG-WARNER CORPORATION (AN ANCESTOR OF BORGWARNER, Inc.) commissioned designer Robert J. Hill and Spaulding-Gorham, Inc., of Chicago, to create a commemorative trophy honoring the winner of the Indianapolis 500.[1]

The design employed an art deco motif popular in the 1930s, including wings on the side that symbolized the speed of flight, but the unique feature was the trophy's base, which displayed sculpted heads of every race winner.

Throughout the years various sculptors have molded the sterling silver images of the race winners' faces, with American sculptor William Behrends creating the likenesses in recent years.

Winners do not get to take the trophy home. It stays on permanent display at the Indianapolis Motor Speedway Museum. Instead, winners and team owners receive sterling silver replicas of the trophy, which is fondly referred to in the racing world as the "Baby Borg." After an image of the winner's head is welded onto the main trophy, a copy is attached to the Baby Borg.

One of the more recognizable trophies in all of sports, the trophy was unveiled at a dinner in New York in February 1936 and featured the bas-relief sculptures of all twenty-four winners up until that time. The new winner has been added every year since. In 1986, the fiftieth anniversary of the trophy, the final space was filled. A base was added in 1987, but it soon became filled. In 2004 a larger version of the base was created with enough spaces to last through the 2034 race.

- 5′ 4.75″ tall with base
- 110 pounds with base
- 80 pounds sterling silver
- Value in 1936: $10,000
- Current value: $3.5 million

FACE THE FACTS

- Louis Meyer was the first driver added to the trophy when he won his third Indianapolis 500 in 1936.
- The youngest driver portrait is of Troy Ruttman (1952), at twenty-two years, 80 days old, and the oldest is Al Unser Sr. (1987), at forty-seven years, 360 days.
- *Oops!* 1950 winner Johnnie Parsons has his first name incorrectly spelled "Johnny."
- Tom Sneva, the 1983 winner, is the only driver on the trophy wearing glasses, at his request.
- There are nine, yes nine, Unser faces on the trophy:
- Bobby Unser—'68, '75, '81
- Al Unser Sr.—'70, '71, '78, '87
- Al Unser Jr.—'92, '94
- There are two sets of drivers' heads for one year on the trophy—cowinners (not two-headed drivers):
- L. L. Corum and Joe Boyer (1924)
- Floyd Davis and Mauri Rose (1941)
- There is one, twenty-four-karat gold head on the trophy. It is that of Tony Hulman, who purchased the track in 1945 and was the owner until he passed away in 1977.[2]

A BRUSH WITH CELEBRITY

- Movies
  1949: *The Big Wheel,* with Mickey Rooney
  1950: *To Please a Lady,* with Barbara Stanwyck and Clark Gable

1969: *Winning*, with Paul Newman, Joanne Woodward, and Robert Wagner

2013: *Turbo*, a 3D computer-animated film from DreamWorks Animation

- Television

1957: The Borg-Warner Trophy appeared on *The Ed Sullivan Show* with Sam Hanks and Cyd Charisse

1967: *The Tonight Show* host Johnny Carson visited the home of the trophy and drove Parnelli Jones's famous STP Turbine at the Indianapolis Motor Speedway.

2004: David Letterman, co-owner of Letterman Rahal Racing, won the Indianapolis 500 with driver Buddy Rice. When Letterman received his Baby Borg, he compared the moment to the thrill he experienced during his first appearance on *The Tonight Show* with Johnny Carson.

2014: The trophy and 2014 Indianapolis 500 winner Ryan Hunter-Reay appeared on *Late Show with David Letterman*.[3]

The trophy travelled to Japan in 2017 in celebration of Takuma Sato's victory the previous May, and in the summer of 2018 it made an appearance at the Goodwood Festival of Speed in England.

The Borg-Warner Trophy.

48

THE BORG-WARNER VICTORY LANE WREATH

DRINKING MILK IN VICTORY LANE. THE PRESENTATION OF THE Borg-Warner Trophy. The singing of "Back Home Again in Indiana." No sporting event boasts more hallowed traditions than the Indianapolis 500. But for winners of the race, perhaps no custom is more cherished than when the Borg-Warner Victory Lane Wreath is placed around their necks. In fact, it's one of the more photographed moments in all of sports.

Inspired by the garlands traditionally bestowed to horse-racing champions, the Borg-Warner Wreath made its debut in 1960.[1] After narrowly beating out Rodger Ward in an epic duel, Jim Rathmann became the first Indianapolis 500 champion to don the wreath, created by famed local florist Bill Cronin. Since then, the wreath has not only become more beautiful but also more imbued with meaning by the few who have been privileged with creating it.

Cronin continued in the role of wreath maker until his passing in 1989. The honor was then bestowed on Dan and Joyce Purifoy of the Festival Florist Shop in Indianapolis for the 1990 and 1991 events. Upon their retirement, the Purifoys turned the duty over to one of their more talented and dedicated employees, Julie Harman Vance. Known to thousands as "the wreath lady," Vance has created every wreath since 1992. Her contributions include standardizing the appearance of the wreath and adding thirty-three orchids to represent every driver in the race.[2]

Vance assembles the wreath at her shop, Buck Creek in Bloom, near Muncie, Indiana. In preparation for assembling the wreath, flowers and foliage are specially ordered from across the country, and only the very best of these are selected for inclusion. In total, the wreath requires seven hours of careful, painstaking work to construct and weighs thirty pounds. "I hope I can build it for as long as I can, or until I can't do it anymore," says Vance.[3]

CONSTRUCTION MATERIALS

- A round, twenty-four-inch Styrofoam base
- Thirty feet of red-white-and-blue-stripped ribbon
- Seventy feet of light-green floral tape
- Thirty-three small water tubes
- Sixty small checkered flags
- 250 steel picks
- One and a half pounds of hot glue

FOLIAGE

- Thirty-three white cymbidium orchids from Oregon
- Cocculus leaves grown in Florida
- Variegated pittosporum leaves from Florida
- Salal leaves grown in Washington State

The only wreath not assembled for presentation in Victory Lane was created to honor two-time Indianapolis 500 champion Dan Wheldon at his memorial tribute in 2011.

BORGWARNER, INC.

BorgWarner, Inc., is a technology leader in highly engineered components and systems for powertrain applications worldwide. BorgWarner, Inc., is also proud to be the official turbocharger supplier to the IndyCar Series.

Because Borg-Warner (as it was then known) commissioned the trophy in 1935, it only seemed natural for the company to assume sponsorship for the wreath as well.

Ryan Hunter-Reay and the Borg-Warner Victory Wreath in 2014.

49

WOMEN IN THE INDIANAPOLIS 500

MAUDE A. YAGLE—MRS. EDWARD YAGLE OF PHILADELPHIA—purchased the 1929 Indianapolis 500 winning car from 1926 winner Frank Lockhart in early 1928. The car finished in fourth place that year with Ray Keech at the wheel. Yagle and Keech returned the following year and won the race. Women were not permitted in the garage area or pit lane at that time, and Yagle was relegated to sitting in a grandstand to track her car throughout the race. A lot has changed since then, though to date, Maude Yagle is the only female owner of a winning car.

In 1977, Janet Guthrie, a thirty-eight-year-old physicist and sports car driver from New York City, became the first woman to qualify for the race. She started in the twenty-sixth positon and finished in the twenty-eighth position.

Nine women, including Guthrie, have participated in the Indianapolis 500. The best finish to date has been Danica Patrick in 2009 when she finished in the third position. Three women have won the coveted Rookie of the Year Award.

Below is a list of the women who have challenged the best drivers in the world on an equal footing.

- Janet Guthrie: 1977–1979
- Lyn St. James: 1992–1997 (Rookie of the Year 1992); 2000
- Sarah Fisher: 2000–2004; 2007–2010
- Danica Patrick: 2005–2011 (Rookie of the Year 2005); 2018
- Milka Duno: 2007–2009

- Ana Beatriz: 2010–2013
- Simona de Silvestro: 2010–2013 (Rookie of the Year 2010); 2015
- Pippa Mann: 2011; 2013–2017
- Katherine Legg: 2012–2013[1]

On three occasions four women have taken the green flag in the same race:

- 2010: Danica Patrick, Sarah Fisher, Ana Beatriz, Simona de Silvestro
- 2011: Danica Patrick, Ana Beatriz, Simona de Silvestro, Pippa Mann
- 2013: Simona de Silvestro, Ana Beatriz, Pippa Mann, Katherine Legge

Maude Yagle would be proud.

50

THE QUILT LADY

JEANETTA PEARSON HOLDER WAS BORN MAY 30, 1932, ON HER FAMILY'S farm near Bowling Green, Kentucky, approximately 225 miles south of the Indianapolis Motor Speedway. This was the same day as the twentieth running of the Indianapolis 500 won by Fred Frame, a race that was notable for the fact that twenty-six of the forty starting cars dropped out of the race due to mechanical issues and accidents.

Holder seemed to be destined to be connected to the Indianapolis 500 and auto racing in general. As a child she made her own race cars using tobacco sticks and lard cans with a nail serving as her shifter.[1]

She also began sewing as a child and made clothes for her doll and pet cat. By the time she was twelve, she had begun making quilts, filling them with cotton she had grown herself.

Holder didn't have a car with which to take her driver's license exam so she borrowed a taxicab. A few years later she could be seen driving a 1950 Hudson around an oval dirt track at Beech Bend Park in Warren County, Kentucky, where she soon earned a reputation for being a determined driver. In 1951 and 1952 she drove a 1935 Chevrolet with a 1950 Mercury engine. At the age of twenty she was one of only a handful of women drivers.

In 1950 Holder attended her first Indianapolis 500, which was won by Johnnie Parsons. She was hooked and would become an avid race fan, collecting autographs from drivers whenever she had a chance.

In the mid-1970s a friend suggested she create a race-themed quilt including the signatures she had acquired, and in 1976 Holder presented a finished quilt to Indianapolis 500 winner Johnny Rutherford.

Rutherford said, "Not only was it the greatest of all thrills to win the Indy 500, but the win became even more special when I became the first

Jeanetta Pearson Holder (center) presents Alexander
Rossi his quilt.

Indy winner to receive one of Jeanetta's exceptional hand-made quilts
created for the Indy winner. I am proud to have the first 'Indy winner
quilt' from such a gracious lady. It is hanging in a place of honor behind
the Indy 500 Pace Cars in my race shop for all to see."[2]

This was just the beginning for Holder. She also honored former winners Jim Rathmann (1960), Parnelli Jones (1963), and Mario Andretti
(1969) with quilts.

The quilt she made for Bobby Unser following his third and final win
in 1981 is part of the Bobby Unser collection at The Henry Ford.

For more than forty years Holder has combined her passion for auto
racing and her talent for making quilts into one of the more unique traditions at the Indianapolis Motor Speedway.

The winning drivers of the Indianapolis 500 treasure these quilts.
Those of Bobby Unser grace the beds in his home, and Rick Mears built
a room in his house to accommodate his four large-sized quilts.[3]

Despite a less-than-easy life, Jeanetta Pearson Holder has endured.
When she speaks of her quilts one can see the pride and satisfaction in
her eyes for contributing to the traditions of the Indianapolis 500-Mile
Race. She is as unique as her quilts.

PART 4

Previous page, 365 days until the next Greatest Spectacle in Racing.

EPILOGUE

The race has been run. The green flag has been waved. A champion has been crowned. And a life has been changed. Forever the winner will be known as an Indianapolis 500 champion, and with that title will come prizes, awards, personal appearances, television and radio interviews, and a host of duties and responsibilities requiring a lifetime to fulfill.

A likeness will be affixed to the Borg-Warner Trophy, books and articles will be written, pictures will be hung on museum walls, and children and grandchildren will forever speak of the exploits of their parent or grandparent with great pride. It is likely the champion will return the following year in hopes of another victory. It will not be to defend the title, however. One does not defend that which can never be taken away.

51

THE 500 VICTORY BANQUET

DATING BACK SEVERAL DECADES, THE TRADITIONAL 500 VICTORY Banquet is held the night after the race. The black-tie celebration was held at the Indiana Convention Center from 1972 through the mid-2000s. More recently it has been held on the grounds of the Indianapolis Motor Speedway.

The banquet was canceled in 1973 due to rain and circumstances surrounding the race. The 1973 race is the one everyone would like to forget. Rain plagued the entire month of May and practice sessions were either delayed or canceled. The start of the race was delayed four hours. An accident involving ten drivers occurred at the start, with David "Salt" Walther suffering a serious but survivable injury. Rain began to fall during the clean-up process so the race was postponed until the following day. On lap 58 David "Swede" Savage experienced a horrific accident that cost him his life. The race was stopped after 133 laps due to more rain. Gordon Johncock was awarded the victory, as the race had passed the minimum of 101 laps. At the end of it all, no one was in a celebratory mood.

Due to rain the 1986 race was delayed until the following Saturday, and the banquet was also canceled. The day after the race, a luncheon was held for the top three finishers at the Speedway Motel. In 2000 and 2001 the affair was held on Sunday night following the race. The banquet was moved back to Monday starting in 2002.

The Victory Banquet is a popular event for drivers, team owners and members, and fans. Each driver is presented his or her prizes, and the driver interviews provide insight into the race the day before.

A most festive evening.

The winning car of the hundredth running of the Indianapolis 500-Mile Race.

Alexander Rossi (at podium) and his team celebrate winning the hundredth running of the Indianapolis 500-Mile Race.

The Borg-Warner Trophy is the most coveted prize in all of motorsports.

52

THE WINNER'S RING

THE WINNING DRIVER OF THE INDIANAPOLIS 500 RECEIVES MANY prizes and awards, but few are as highly coveted or valued as the Winner's Ring.

In 1983, Ken Keltner of Herff-Jones was asked to create a ring for the Indianapolis 500 winner. The ring is fourteen-karat yellow gold with twelve genuine diamonds, weighing a total of one carat, adorning the top in the shape of the Indianapolis Motor Speedway. On one side of the ring is the official logo of the Indianapolis Motor Speedway, the famed Wing and Wheel, along with the year and the anniversary date of the race. The other side has the Borg-Warner Trophy along with the winner's name and car number. The ring is copyrighted by the Indianapolis Motor Speedway and recently has been appraised at more than $9,000.

The first to receive this one-of-a-kind creation was Tom "The Gas Man" Sneva. Herff-Jones also provided rings for winning car owners, starters, the pit-stop champions' crews, and the official fan ring.[1]

In 2017, it was announced Jostens would be the new jewelry and trophy provider of the Indianapolis Motor Speedway. Founded in 1897 and based in Minneapolis, Jostens has produced championship rings for colleges and professional teams for more than sixty years.

J. Douglas Boles, president of Indianapolis Motor Speedway said, "These rings are a special part of racing history, celebrating one of the greatest victories in all of sports and forming a lifelong keepsake for some of our most celebrated drivers."[2]

Dan Wheldon was the winner of the hundredth anniversary race.

53

A LIFETIME OF MEMORIES

THE CROWD HAS GONE. THE DRIVERS, CARS, TEAMS, AND OFFICIALS are making their way to the next race. But for all those who witnessed or took part in the Great Race, there will be memories. Whether it was someone's first race or fiftieth, there will be memories lasting a lifetime, and for many those memories will fuel a passion for the Indianapolis 500.

Meanwhile, she waits in silence in all her grandeur. The Indianapolis Motor Speedway, the greatest race course in the world, will wait patiently until next May and the next Greatest Spectacle in Racing. As said by Indianapolis Motor Speedway chairman of the board Tony George,

"This is no mere racetrack;
This is a temple.
This is the most hallowed ground in motorsports.
This is *Indy!*"[1]

Appendix

1911–12 program cover.

Table 01. Indianapolis 500-Mile Race Champions

Year	SP	Car No.	Driver(s)	Car Name/Entrant Chassis/Engine	Qual. Speed	Race Time	Race Speed
1911	28	32	Ray Harroun	Nordyke & Marmon/Marmon/Marmon	N/A	6:42:08.000	74.602
1912	7	8	Joe Dawson	National Motor Vehicle/National/National	86.130	6:21:06.000	78.719
1913	7	16	Jules Goux	Peugeot/Peugeot/Peugeot	86.030	6:35:05.000	75.933
1914	15	16	Rene Thomas	L. Delage/Delage/Delage	94.540	6:03:45.000	82.474
1915	2	2	Ralph DePalma	Mercedes/E. C. Patterson/Mercedes/Mercedes	98.580	5:33:55.510	89.840
1916	4	17	Dario Resta	Peugeot Auto Racing/Peugeot/Peugeot	94.400	3:34:17.000	84.001
1919	2	3	Howdy Wilcox	Peugeot/Indianapolis Speedway Team/Peugeot/Peugeot	100.010	5:40:42.870	88.050
1920	6	4	Gaston Chevrolet	Monroe/William Small/Frontenac/Frontenac	91.550	5:38:32.000	88.618
1921	20	2	Tommy Milton	Frontenac/Louis Chevrolet/Frontenac/Frontenac	93.050	5:34:44.650	89.621
1922	1	35	Jimmy Murphy	Jimmy Murphy/Duesenberg/Miller	100.500	5:17:30.790	94.484
1923	1	1	Tommy Milton	H. C. S. Motor/Miller/Miller	108.170	5:29:50.170	90.954
1924	21	15	L. L. Corum J. Boyer	Duesenberg/Duesenberg/Duesenberg	93.330	5:05:23.510	98.234
1925	2	12	Peter DePaolo	Duesenberg/Duesenberg/Duesenberg	113.080	4:56:39.460	101.127
1926	20	15	Frank Lockhart	Miller/Peter Kreis/Miller/Miller	95.780	4:10:14.950	95.904
1927	22	32	George Souders	Duesenberg/William White/Duesenberg/Duesenberg	111.550	5:07:33.080	97.545
1928	13	14	Louis Meyer	Miller/Alden Sampson II/Miller/Miller	111.350	5:01:33.750	99.482
1929	6	2	Ray Keech	Simplex Piston Ring/Yagle/Miller/Miller	114.900	5:07:25.420	97.585
1930	1	4	Billy Arnold	Miller-Hartz/Summers/Miller	113.260	4:58:39.720	100.448
1931	13	23	Louis Schneider	Bowes Seal Fast/Schneider/Stevens/Miller	107.210	5:10:27.930	96.629

1932	27	34	Fred Frame	Miller-Harry Hartz/Wetteroth/Miller	113.850	4:48:03.790	104.144
1933	6	36	Louis Meyer	Tydol/Louis Meyer/Miller/Miller	116.970	4:48:00.750	104.162
1934	10	7	Bill Cummings	Boyle Products/Henning/Miller/Miller	116.110	4:46:05.200	104.863
1935	22	5	Kelly Petillo	Gilmore Speedway/Petillo/Wetteroth/Offy	115.090	4:42:22.710	106.240
1936	28	8	Louis Meyer	Ring Free/Louis Meyer Stevens/Miller	114.170	4:35:03.390	109.069
1937	2	6	Wilbur Shaw	Shaw-Gilmore/Shaw/Offy	122.790	4:24:07.800	113.580
1938	1	23	Floyd Roberts	Burd Piston Ring/Lou Moore/Wetteroth/Miller	125.680	4:15:58.400	117.200
1939	3	2	Wilbur Shaw	Boyle Racing Headquarters/Maserati/Maserati	128.970	4:20:47.390	115.035
1940	2	1	Wilbur Shaw	Boyle Racing Headquarters/Maserati/Maserati	127.060	4:22:31.170	114.277
1941	17	16	Floyd Davis / Mauri Rose	Noc-Out Hose Clamp/Moore/Wetteroth/Offy	121.100	4:20:36.240	115.117
1946	15	16	George Robson	Thorne Engineering/ Adams/Sparks	125.540	4:21:16.700	114.820
1947	3	27	Mauri Rose	Blue Crown Spark Plug/Moore/Deidt/Offy	120.040	4:17:52.170	116.338
1948	3	3	Mauri Rose	Blue Crown Spark Plug/Moore/Deidt/Offy	129.120	4:10:23.330	119.814
1949	4	7	Bill Holland	Blue Crown Spark Plug/Moore/Deidt/Offy	128.670	4:07:15.970	121.327
1950	5	1	Johnnie Parsons	Wynn's Friction/Kurtis-Kraft/Kurtis/Offy	132.040	2:46:55.970	124.002
1951	2	99	Lee Wallard	Murrell Belanger/Kurtis/Offy	135.030	3:57:38.050	126.244
1952	7	98	Troy Ruttman	J. C. Agajanian/Kuzma/Offy	135.360	3:52:41.880	128.922
1953	1	14	Bill Vukovich	Fuel Injection/Howard Keck KK500A/Offy	138.390	3:53:01.690	128.740
1954	19	14	Bill Vukovich	Fuel Injection/Howard Keck KK500A/Offy	138.470	3:49:17.270	130.840
1955	14	6	Bob Sweikert	John Zink KK500C/Offy	139.990	3:53:59.130	128.213
1956	1	8	Pat Flaherty	John Zink/Watson/Offy	145.590	3:53:28.840	128.490

(Continued)

Table 01. *Continued*

Year	SP	Car No.	Driver(s)	Car Name/Entrant Chassis/Engine	Qual. Speed	Race Time	Race Speed
1957	13	9	Sam Hanks	Belond Exhaust/George Salih/Salih/Offy	142.810	3:41:14.250	135.601
1958	7	1	Jimmy Bryan	Belond AP/George Salih/Salih/Offy	144.180	3:44:13.800	133.791
1959	6	5	Rodger Ward	Leader Card 500 Roadster/Watson/Offy	144.030	3:40:49.200	135.857
1960	2	4	Jim Rathmann	Ken-Paul/Watson/Offy	146.370	3:36:11.360	138.767
1961	7	1	A. J. Foyt	Bowes Seal Fast/Bignotti Trevis/Offy	145.900	3:35:37.490	139.130
1962	2	3	Rodger Ward	Leader Card 500 Roadster/Watson/Offy	149.370	3:33:50.330	140.293
1963	1	98	Parnelli Jones	J. C. Agajanian/Willard Battery Watson/Offy	151.150	3:29:35.400	143.137
1964	5	1	A. J. Foyt	Sheraton-Thompson/Ansted Watson/Offy	154.670	3:23:35.830;	147.350
1965	2	82	Jim Clark	Lotus powered by Ford/Lotus/Ford	160.720	3:19:05.340	150.686
1966	15	24	Graham Hill	American Red Ball/Mecom Lola/Ford	159.240	3:27:52.530	144.317
1967	4	14	A. J. Foyt	Sheraton-Thompson/Ansted Coyote/Ford	166.280	3:18:24.220	151.207
1968	3	3	Bobby Unser	Rislone/Leader Cards/Eagle/Offy	169.500	3:16:13.760	152.882
1969	2	2	Mario Andretti	STP Oil Treatment/Hawk/Ford	169.850	3:11:14.710	156.867
1970	1	2	Al Unser Sr.	Johnny Lightning/Parnelli Jones/P. J. Colt/Ford	170.220	3:12:37.040	155.749
1971	5	1	Al Unser Sr.	Johnny Lightning/Parnelli Jones/P. J. Colt/Ford	174.520	3:10:11.560	157.735
1972	3	66	Mark Donohue	Sunoco McLaren/Penske/McLaren/Offy	191.400	3:04:05.540	162.962
1973	11	20	Gordon Johncock	STP Double Oil Filter/Patrick Eagle/Offy	192.550	2:05:26.590	159.036
1974	25	3	Johnny Rutherford	McLaren Cars/McLaren/Offy	190.440	3:09:10.060	158.589
1975	3	48	Bobby Unser	Jorgensen/All American Racers Eagle/Offy	191.070	2:54:55.080	149.213

Year			Driver	Entrant/Chassis/Engine			
1976	1	2	Johnny Rutherford	Hy-Gain/McLaren/McLaren/Offy	188.950	1:42:52.000	148.725
1977	4	14	A.J. Foyt	Gilmore Racing/A.J. Foyt	194.560	3:05:57.160	161.331
1978	5	2	Al Unser Sr.	First National City/Chaparral	196.470	3:05:54.990	161.363
1979	1	9	Rick Mears	The Gould Charge/Penske/Penske/Cosworth	193.730	3:08:47.970	158.899
1980	1	4	Johnny Rutherford	Pennzoil/Chaparral Racing/Chaparral/Cosworth	192.520	3:29:59.560	142.862
1981	1	3	Bobby Unser	The Norton Spirit/Penske/Penske/Cosworth	200.540	3:35:41.780	139.084
1982	5	20	Gordon Johncock	STP Oil Treatment/Patrick Wildcat/Cosworth	201.880	3:05:09.140	162.029
1983	4	5	Tom Sneva	Texaco Star/Bignotti-Cotter/March/Cosworth	203.680	3:05:03.066	162.117
1984	3	6	Rick Mears	Pennzoil Z-7/Penske/March/Cosworth	207.840	3:03:21.660	163.612
1985	8	5	Danny Sullivan	Miller American/Penske/March/Cosworth	210.290	3:16:06.069	152.982
1986	4	3	Bobby Rahal	Budweiser/Truesports/March/Cosworth	213.550	2:55:43.480	170.722
1987	20	25	Al Unser Sr.	Cummins-Holset/Penske/March/Cosworth	207.420	3:04:59.147	162.175
1988	1	5	Rick Mears	Pennzoil Z-7/Penske/Penske/Chevy Indy V8	219.190	3:27:10.204	144.809
1989	3	20	Emerson Fittipaldi	Marlboro/Patrick Racing/Penske/Chevy Indy V8	222.320	2:59:01.049	167.581
1990	3	30	Arie Luyendyk	Domino's Pizza/Shierson—Lola/Chevy Indy V8	223.300	2:41:18.404	185.981i
1991	1	3	Rick Mears	Marlboro Penske Chevy 91/Penske/Chevy Indy V8	224.113	2:50:00.791	176.457
1992	12	3	Al Unser Jr.	Valvoline Galmer '92/Galmer/Chevy Indy V8A	222.989	3:43:05.148	134.477
1993	9	4	Emerson Fittipaldi	Marlboro Penske Chevy '93/Penske/Chevy Indy V8C	220.150	3:10:49.860	157.207
1994	1	31	Al Unser Jr.	Marlboro Penske Mercedes/Penske/Mercedes Benz	228.011	3:06:29.006	160.872
1995	5	27	Jacques Villeneuve	Player's LTD/Team Green Reynard/Ford Cosworth XB	228.397	3:15:17.561	153.616

(Continued)

Table 01. *Continued*

Year	SP	Car No.	Driver(s)	Car Name/Entrant Chassis/Engine	Qual. Speed	Race Time	Race Speed
1996	5	91	Buddy Lazier	Delta Faucet/Montana/Hemelgarn 95 Reynard/Ford Cosworth XB	231.468	3:22:45.753	147.956
1997	1	5	Arie Luyendyk	Wavephore/Sprint PCS/Miller Lite/Provimi/G Force/Aurora	218.263	3:25:43.388	145.827
1998	17	51	Eddie Cheever Jr.	Rachel's Potato Chips/Dallara/Aurora	217.334	3:26:40.524	145.155
1999	8	14	Kenny Brack	A. J. Foyt PowerTeam Racing/Dallara/Aurora	222.659	3:15:51.182	153.176
2000	2	9	Juan Pablo Montoya	Target/G Force Oldsmobile /td>	223.372	2:58:59.431	167.607
2001	11	68	Helio Castroneves	Marlboro Team Penske/Dallara/Oldsmobile	224.142	3:31:54.180	141.574
2002	13	3	Helio Castroneves	Marlboro Team Penske/Dallara/Chevy	229.052	3:00:10.8714	166.499
2003	10	6	Gil de Ferran	Marlboro Team Penske/G Force/Toyota	228.633	3:11:56.9891	156.291
2004	1	15	Buddy Rice	Rahal Letterman Racing/Panoz G Force/Honda	222.024	3:14:55.2395	138.518
2005	16	26	Dan Wheldon	Andretti Green Racing/Dallara/Honda	224.308	3:10:21.0769	157.603
2006	1	6	Sam Hornish Jr.	Marlboro Team Penske/Dallara/Honda	228.985	3:10:58.7590	157.085
2007	3	27	Dario Franchitti	Andretti Green Racing/Dallara/Honda	225.191	2:44:03.5608	151.774
2008	1	9	Scott Dixon	Target Chip Ganassi Racing/Dallara/Honda	226.366	3:28:57.6792	143.567
2009	1	3	Helio Castroneves	Team Penske/Dallara/Honda	224.864	3:19:34.6427	150.318
2010	3	9	Dario Franchitti	Target Chip Ganassi Racing/Dallara/Honda	226.990	3:05:37.0131	161.623
2011	6	98	Dan Wheldon	Bryan Herta Autosport with Curb/Agajanian/Dallara/Honda	226.490	2:56:11.7267	170.265

Year			Driver	Team/Chassis/Engine			
2012	16	50	Dario Franchitti	Target Chip Ganassi Racing/Dallara/Honda	223.582	2:58:51.2532	167.734
2013	12	11	Tony Kanaan	KV Racing Technology/Dallara/Chevrolet	226.949	2:40:03.4181	187.433
2014	19	28	Ryan Hunter-Reay	DHL Honda/Dallara/Honda	229.719	2:40:48.2305	186.563
2015	15	2	Juan Pablo Montoya	Verizon Team Penske Chevrolet/Dallara/Chevrolet	224.657	3:05:56.5286	161.341
2016	11	98	Alexander Rossi	NAPA Autosports/Andretti Herta Autosport/Dallara/Curb Honda	228.473	3:00:02.0872	166.634
2017	4	26	Takuma Sato	Andretti Autosport/Dallara/Honda	231.365	3:13:03.3584	155.395
2018	3	12	Will Power	Verizon Team Penske Chevrolet	228.607	2:59:42.6365	166.935

"Indianapolis Motor Speedway Indianapolis 500 Winners," Indianapolis Motor Speedway, accessed October 6, 2018, http://www .indianapolismotorspeedway.com/events/indy500/history/historical-stats/race-stats/summaries/indianapolis-500-race-winners.

Table 02. Indianapolis 500-Mile Race Records

Laps	Miles	Time	Speed	Driver	Entrant Name	Year
1	2.5	41.3359	217.728	Tony Kanaan	Andretti Green Racing	2007
2	5	1:21.094	221.965	Tony Stewart	Team Menard	1996
4	10	2:43.771	219.819	Helio Castroneves	Marlboro Team Penske	2003
10	25	6:45.77841	221.703	Tony Kanaan	Andretti Green Racing	2005
20	50	13:36.011	220.585	Bruno Junqueira	Target/Chip Ganassi	2002
30	75	20:43.090	217.201	Bruno Junqueira	Target/Chip Ganassi	2002
40	100	28:15.646	212.308	Will Power	Team Penske	2014
50	125	35:14.1823	212.848	Will Power	Team Penske	2014
60	150	42:12.2288	213.251	Marco Andretti	Andretti Autosport	2014
70	175	49:41.5486	211.300	Helio Castroneves	Team Penske	2014
80	200	56:32.6565	212.223	Helio Castroneves	Team Penske	2014
90	225	1:03:21.4821	213.075	Helio Castroneves	Team Penske	2014
100	250	1:10:47.8745	211.871	Ryan Hunter-Reay	Andretti Autosport	2014
110	275	1:17:37.1795	212.575	Helio Castroneves	Team Penske	2014
120	300	1:24:24.0448	213.268	Ryan Hunter-Reay	Andretti Autosport	2014
130	325	1:31:17.6531	213.595	Juan Pablo Montoya	Team Penske	2014
140	350	1:38:42.8021	212.737	Marco Andretti	Andretti Autosport	2014
150	375	1:45:51.7817	212.539	Marco Andretti	Andretti Autosport	2014
160	400	1:58:29.5150	202.543	Ryan Hunter-Reay	Andretti Autosport	2014
170	425	2:06:41.8255	201.267	Ryan Hunter-Reay	Andretti Autosport	2014
180	450	2:20:41.0338	191.920	Carlos Munoz	Andretti Autosport	2013
190	475	2:28:09.0402	192.372	Ryan Hunter-Reay	Andretti Autosport	2013
200	500	2:40:03.4181	187.433	Tony Kanaan	KV Racing Technology	2013

"Indianapolis Motor Speedway Indianapolis 500 Race Records," Indianapolis Motor Speedway, accessed October 6, 2018, http://www.indianapolismotorspeedway.com/events/indy500/history/historical-stats/race-stats/summaries/track-records-race.

Tony Kanaan is the winner of the fastest Indianapolis 500-Mile Race in history.

Table 03. Indianapolis 500-Mile Race Qualifying Records

Laps	Miles	Time	Speed	Driver	Entrant Name	Year
1	2.5	37.895	237.498	Arie Luyendyk	Byrd-Treadway Racing	1996
4	10	2:31.908	236.986	Arie Luyendyk	Byrd-Treadway Racing	1996

"Indianapolis 500 Historical Stats," Indianapolis Motor Speedway, accessed October 6, 2018, http://www.indianapolismotorspeedway .com/events/indy500/history/historical-stats/race-stats/records /track-records-qualifications.

The Byrd-Treadway racing machine with Arie Luyendyk at the wheel is the fastest car in the history of the Indianapolis 500-Mile Race.

Table 04. Indianapolis 500-Mile Race Broken Speed Barriers—Qualifications

Barrier	Driver	Engine	Speed (mph)	Year
100 mph	Rene Thomas	Delage	104.785	1919
110 mph	Earl Cooper	Miller	110.728	1925
120 mph	Frank Lockhart	Miller	120.546	1927
130 mph	Jimmy Snyder	Sparks	130.492	1937
140 mph	Jack McGrath	Offenhauser	141.287	1954
150 mph	Parnelli Jones	Offenhauser	150.729	1962
160 mph	Jim Clark	Ford	160.973	1965
170 mph	Graham Hill	Pratt & Whitney	171.887	1968
180 mph	Billy Vukovich	Offenhauser	185.797	1972
190 mph	Bobby Unser	Offenhauser	196.678	1972
200 mph	Tom Sneva	Cosworth	200.535	1977
210 mph	Tom Sneva	Cosworth	210.689	1984
220 mph	Rick Mears	Chevy Indy V8	220.453	1988
230 mph	Roberto Guerrero	Buick	232.618	1992

"Indianapolis Motor Speedway Broken Speed Barriers—Qualifications," Indianapolis Motor Speedway, accessed October 6, 2018, https://www .indianapolismotorspeedway.com/events/indy500/history/historical-stats /race-stats/records/broken-speed-barriers.

Table 05. Indianapolis 500-Mile Race Pace Cars and Drivers

Year	Pace Car	Driver
1911	Stoddard-Dayton	Carl G. Fisher
1912	Stutz	Carl G. Fisher
1913	Stoddard-Dayton	Carl G. Fisher
1914	Stoddard-Dayton	Carl G. Fisher
1915	Packard 6 (Model 5-48)	Carl G. Fisher
1916	Premier 6 (Model6-56)	Frank E. Smith
1919	Packard V12 (Twin Six)	Colonel Jesse G. Vincent
1920	Marmon 6 (Model 34)	Barney Oldfield
1921	H. C. S. 6	Harry C. Stutz
1922	National Sextet	Barney Oldfield
1923	Duesenberg	Fred S. Duesenberg
1924	Cole V8	Lew Petti john
1925	Rickenbacker 8	Captain Eddie Rickenbacker
1926	Chrysler Imperial 80	Louis Chevrolet
1927	LaSalle V8	Willard "Big Boy" Rader
1928	Marmon 8 (Model 78)	Joe Dawson
1929	Studebaker President	George Hunt
1930	Cord L-29	Wade Morton
1931	Cadillac	Willard "Big Boy" Rader
1932	Lincoln	Edsel Ford
1933	Chrysler Imperial (Phaeton)	Byron Foy
1934	LaSalle	Willard "Big Boy" Rader
1935	Ford V-8	Harry Mack
1936	Packard 120	Tommy Milton
1937	LaSalle	Ralph DePalma
1938	Hudson 112	Stuart Baits
1939	Buick Roadmaster 80 Series	Charles Chayne
1940	Studebaker Champion	Ab Jenkins
1941	Chrysler-Newport (Phaeton)	A. B. Couture
1946	Lincoln Continental	Henry Ford II
1947	Nash Ambassador	George W. Mason
1948	Chevrolet Stylemaster Six-Series	Wilbur Shaw
1949	Oldsmobile 88	Wilbur Shaw
1950	Mercury	Benson Ford
1951	Chrysler New Yorker	Dave Wallace
1952	Studebaker Commander	P.O. Peterson

(*Continued*)

Table 05. *Continued*

Year	Pace Car	Driver
1953	Ford Crestline Sunliner	William Clay Ford Sr.
1954	Dodge Royal 500	William C. Newburg
1955	Chevrolet Bel Air	Thomas H. Keating
1956	DeSoto Fireflight	L. I. Woolson
1957	Mercury	F. C. "Jack" Reith
1958	Pontiac Bonneville	Sam Hanks
1959	Buick Electra 225	Sam Hanks
1960	Oldsmobile 98	Sam Hanks
1961	Ford Thunderbird	Sam Hanks
1962	Studebaker Lark Daytona	Sam Hanks
1963	Chrysler 300	Sam Hanks
1964	Ford Mustang	Benson Ford
1965	Plymouth Sports Fury	P. M. Buckminster
1966	Mercury Comet Cyclone GT	Benson Ford
1967	Chevrolet Camaro RS/SS	Mauri Rose
1968	Ford Torino/Fairlane	William Clay Ford Sr.
1969	Chevrolet Camaro	Jim Rathmann
1970	Oldsmobile 4-4-2	Rodger Ward
1971	Dodge Challenger	Eldon Palmer
1972	Hurst-Olds Cutlass	Jim Rathmann
1973	Cadillac Eldorado	Jim Rathmann
1974	Hurst-Olds Cutlass	Jim Rathmann
1975	Buick Century Custom	James Garner
1976	Buick Century	Marty Robbins
1977	Oldsmobile Delta 88	James Garner
1978	Chevrolet Corvette	Jim Rathmann
1979	Ford Mustang II	Jackie Stewart
1980	Pontiac Turbo-Trans Am	Johnnie Parsons Sr.
1981	Buick Regal	Duke Nalon
1982	Chevrolet Camaro Z-28	Jim Rathman
1983	Buick Riviera Convertible	Duke Nalon
1984	Pontiac Fiero	John Callies
1985	Oldsmobile Calais	James Garner
1986	Chevrolet Corvette	Gen. Chuck Yeager
1987	Chrysler LeBaron	Carroll Shelby
1988	Oldsmobile Cutlass Supreme	General Chuck Yeager
1989	Pontiac Trans AM GTA	Bobby Unser

(Continued)

Table 05. *Continued*

Year	Pace Car	Driver
1990	Chevrolet Beretta	Jim Perkins
1991	Dodge Viper	Carroll Shelby
1992	Cadillac Allanté	Bobby Unser
1993	Chevrolet Camaro Z-28	Jim Perkins
1994	Ford Mustang Cobra	Parnelli Jones
1995	Chevrolet Corvette	Jim Perkins
1996	Dodge Viper	Robert A. Lutz
1997	Oldsmobile Aurora	Johnny Rutherford
1998	Chevrolet Corvette	Parnelli Jones
1999	Chevrolet Monte Carlo	Jay Leno
2000	Oldsmobile Aurora	Anthony Edwards
2001	Oldsmobile Bravada	Elaine Irwin-Mellencamp
2002	Chevrolet Corvette	Jim Caviezel
2003	Chevy SSR	Herb Fishel
2004	Chevrolet Corvette C5	Morgan Freeman
2005	Chevrolet Corvette	Gen. Colin Powell
2006	Chevrolet Corvette Z-06	Lance Armstrong
2007	Chevrolet Corvette Convertible	Patrick Dempsey
2008	Chevrolet Corvette Z-06	Emerson Fittipaldi
2009	Chevrolet Camaro	Josh Duhamel
2010	Chevrolet Camaro SS	Robin Roberts
2011	Chevrolet Camaro SS Convertible	A. J. Foyt
2012	Chevrolet Corvette ZR1	Guy Fieri
2013	2014 Chevrolet Corvette C7 Stingray	Jim Harbaugh
2014	Chevrolet Camaro Z/28	Dario Franchitti
2015	2015 Chevrolet Corvette Z06	Jeff Gordon
2016	50th Anniversary Chevrolet Camaro SS	Roger Penske
2017	Chevrolet Corvette Grand Sport	Jeffrey Dean Morgan
2018	Chevrolet Corvette ZR1	Victor Oladipo

"Indy 500 Pace Cars," IndyMotorSpeedway.com, accessed September 20, 2018, http://indymotorspeedway.com/v1/500pace.htm.

WHEN THE INDIANAPOLIS MOTOR SPEEDWAY OPENED

The Indianapolis Motor Speedway officially opened on June 5, 1909, with gas-filled balloon races. Below are a few major events, cultural happenings, and other facts and figures from 1909.

World and National Events

- William Howard Taft succeeded Theodore Roosevelt as president of the United States in March.
- The National Association for the Advancement of Colored People (NAACP) is founded.
- Robert Peary, Matthew Henson, and four Eskimo explorers allegedly reach the North Pole.
- Ernest Shackleton's expedition claims to have found the magnetic South Pole.
- Alice Huyler Ramsey, a twenty-two-year-old housewife from Hackensack, NJ, becomes the first woman to drive across the United States. The thirty-eight-hundred-mile trip, from New York to San Francisco, takes fifty-nine days.
- Louis Bleriot becomes the first man to fly across the English Channel.
- Construction begins on the RMS *Titanic*.

Area Events

- The federal government filed a libel suit against the *Indianapolis News* when the newspaper questioned Theodore Roosevelt's work on the Panama Canal deal. The editors were indicted but refused to be tried in Washington, saying the trial should take place in Indianapolis, where the alleged libel took place. The judge ruled in favor of the *News*. It was a landmark ruling for freedom of the press that still stands.

Area Government

- Indiana US Senators: Albert J. Beveridge, Republican; James A. Hemenway, Republican (until March 1909); Benjamin F. Shively, Democrat (after March 1909)
- Indiana Governor: Thomas R. Marshall, Democrat
- Indianapolis Mayor: Charles A. Bookwalter, Republican

Population Facts and Figures

- World population: 1.7 billion (7.5 billion in 2018)[1]
- US population: 90 million (327 million in 2018)[2]
- Indianapolis population: 233,650 (838,000 in 2018)[3]
- Median age of US population: 24.1 (37.8 in 2018)[4]

Nobel Prize Winners

- Physics: Ferdinand Braun, Guglielmo Marconi
- Chemistry: Wilhelm Ostwald
- Medicine: Emil Theodor Kocher
- Literature: Selma Lagerlof
- Peace: Auguste Marie Francois Beernaert, Paul-Henri-Benjamin d'Estournelles de Constant

Select Consumer Prices

- First-class stamp: two cents
- Hershey's milk chocolate bar: two cents
- Bottle of Coca-Cola: five cents
- Gallon of gas: six cents
- Box of Kellogg's Corn Flakes: ten cents
- New car (average): $1,280
- New home (average): $2,650
- $1.00 had the same purchasing power as $27.74 in 2018[5]

Sports Champions

- World Series: Pittsburgh Pirates
- Stanley Cup: Ottawa Hockey Club (Senators)
- Kentucky Derby: Wintergreen
- NCAA football: Yale
- Heavyweight boxing world champion: Jack Johnson, United States
- AAA auto racing national champion: George Robertson[6]

The Indianapolis Motor Speedway celebrated one hundred years of worldwide leadership in motorsports entertainment from 2009 to 2011 through its centennial era, which featured many special events and a retro corporate logo. Plans for the centennial era celebration were revealed during an event on May 22, 2008, at Allison Mansion of Marian College in Indianapolis.

IMS honored the hundredth anniversaries of the opening of the venerable racetrack in 1909 and the inaugural Indianapolis 500 in 1911 through the centennial era celebration.

"No other motorsports facility in the world has the rich history and tradition of the Indianapolis Motor Speedway," IMS Chairman of the Board Mari Hulman-George said. "The centennial era celebration pays homage to the heroes and events of our storied past while anticipating an even more glorious future."[7]

Centennial Gala

The Centennial Gala took place February 27, 2009, at the Indiana Convention Center in downtown Indianapolis. Nineteen of the twenty-seven living Indianapolis 500 winners—including four-time winners A. J. Foyt, Al Unser Sr., and Rick Mears—were among the featured guests at the black-tie event. Proceeds benefited the Indianapolis Motor Speedway Foundation, which operates the Indianapolis Motor Speedway Museum.

Centennial Era Balloon Festival

The Centennial Era Balloon Festival presented by AT&T Yellow Pages took place May 1–3, 2009, at IMS, with a full schedule of evening balloon "glows" and daytime ascensions. The event returned May 8, 2010. Both events commemorated the first competitive event ever at the speedway, a gas-filled balloon race June 5, 1909.[8]

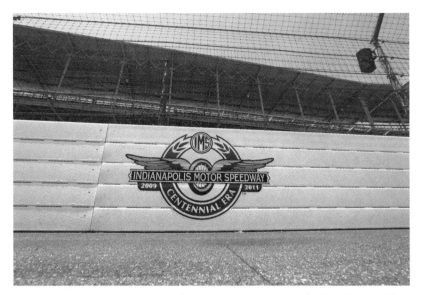

A new Centennial Era logo was used at IMS from 2009–2011. The logo, designed by IMS Creative Services, drew upon elements from 1909, 1934, and 1961 graphics in a historic motif.

THE FANS

Each and every year, hundreds of thousands of fans pass through the gates of the Indianapolis Motor Speedway to witness the Indianapolis 500-Mile Race. They are the lifeblood of the World's Greatest Race Course and the Greatest Spectacle in Racing. Without them neither would exist. Some have made the pilgrimage for forty, fifty, or sixty or more years in a row. They are the most passionate fans of any sporting venue or sporting event in the world, embracing the history, heritage, and traditions of the Indianapolis Motor Speedway and the Indianapolis 500-Mile Race.

A most exciting day lies ahead!

The excitement builds!

APPENDIX

The largest single-day sporting event in the world.

Notes

PART 1

1. Leslie Bailey, "The Stories Behind Your Favorite Indianapolis 500 Traditions," *IndyStar*, May 1, 2014, https://www.indystar.com/story /entertainment/2014/05/01/indy-500-traditions/8561391/.

2. Indianapolis Motor Speedway Centennial Era, *The Spirit of the Indianapolis Motor Speedway*, 2009, video. This moving, 3 minute 51 second video highlighting the history of the Indianapolis 500-Mile Race was originally shown at the Inaugural Centennial Era Gala. It can be found on the IMS YouTube channel at https:// www.youtube.com/watch?v=orN97dsoUjY (accessed September 12, 2018).

CHAPTER 2

1. Donald Davidson and Rick Shaffer, *Autocourse Official History of The Indianapolis 500*, 2nd ed. (Worcestershire, UK: Icon Publishing Limited, 2013).

CHAPTER 3

1. Donald Davidson, *Indianapolis Motor Speedway: A History* (Indianapolis, IN: Indianapolis Motor Speedway Museum, 1956).

CHAPTER 4

1. George Phillips, "The Origins of the IMS Yellow Shirt," *Oil Pressure* (blog), May 7, 2013, https://oilpressure.wordpress.com/2013/05/07 /the-origins-of-the-ims-yellow-shirt/.

CHAPTER 5

1. "Yard of Bricks & Pagoda," Indianapolis Motor Speedway, accessed September 12, 2018, http://www.indianapolismotorspeedway.com/at-the-track /yard-of-bricks-pagoda/the-pagoda.

CHAPTER 6

1. Jeremy Riffle and Suzi Elliott, *Fact Sheet* (Indianapolis, IN: The Indianapolis Motor Speedway Media Center, 2014). This fact sheet was produced for guests of the Indianapolis Motor Speedway Museum and employees of the Indianapolis Motor Speedway.

CHAPTER 7

1. Amanda Bell, "Mom Unser's Chili: A Hot Indy 500 Tradition," *IndyStar*, May 1, 2014, https://www.indystar.com/story/life/food/2014/05/01/mom-unsers-chili-hot-indy-tradition/8577767/.

CHAPTER 9

1. "Plan Your Visit," Indianapolis Motor Speedway Museum, accessed September 12, 2018, indyracingmuseum.org/plan-your-visit.

CHAPTER 10

1. Steve Habel, "Indy's Brickyard Crossing Has Unique Setting and Plenty to Like," *Golf Daily*, May 14, 2018, http://www.cybergolf.com/golf_news/brickyard_crossing_has_unique_setting_much_to_like.

CHAPTER 11

1. Donald Davidson and Rick Shaffer, *Autocourse Official History of the Indianapolis 500*, 2nd ed. (Worcestershire, UK: Icon Publishing Limited, 2013).

CHAPTER 12

1. "Carnegie Retiring after 61 Years as Voice of the Speedway," *USA Today*, June 14, 2006, https://usatoday30.usatoday.com/sports/motor/irl/2006-06-14-carnegie-retirement_x.htm.

2. Nelson Price, "He's On It," *Traces of Indiana and Midwestern History* (Indianapolis: Indiana Historical Society, 2015), 27 (1): 14–21.

3. Linda Weintraut and Jane Nolan, "In the Public Interest," *Oral Histories of Hoosier Broadcasters* (Indianapolis: Indiana Historical Society, 1999), 110–120.

4. "The Tom Carnegie Legacy," Indianapolis Motor Speedway, accessed June 18, 2018, http://www.indianapolismotorspeedway.com/events/indy500/history/tom-carnegie-legacy.

CHAPTER 13

1. Brett Hickman, "'Mr. First in Line' of the Indy 500." *The Southsider Voice*, January 1, 2016, http://www.southsidervoice.com/car-nutz

/mr-first-in-line-of-the-indy-500; Brian Schmitz, "Gates May Be Closing on Indy 500 Tradition," *Orlando Sentinel*, May 12, 1987, http://articles.orlandosentinel .com/1987-05-12/sports/0130070041_1_bisceglia-first-in-line-indy.

CHAPTER 14

1. "Indy 500 Traditions and FAQs," Indianapolis Motor Speedway, accessed September 21, 2018. http://www.indianapolismotorspeedway.com/events /indy500/history/indy-500-traditions-faqs/traditions.

CHAPTER 15

1. "Older Indy 500 Qualifying History," IndySpeedway, accessed September 12, 2018, http://indymotorspeedway.com/qualifying.html#indy500; Donald Davidson and Rick Shaffer, *Autocourse Official History of the Indianapolis 500*, 2nd ed. (Worcestershire, UK: Icon Publishing Limited, 2013); Pat Kennedy, *Indy 500 Recaps: The Short Chute Edition* (Bloomington, IN: AuthorHouse, 2012).

CHAPTER 16

1. "IRL: IMS Presents Indianapolis 500 Traditions," Motorsport.com, May 3, 2006, https://www.motorsport.com/us/indycar/news /irl-ims-presents-indianapolis-500-traditions/2082202/.
2. "$50,000 and Bragging Rights on Line at Tag Heuer Pit Stop Challenge," Indianapolis Motor Speedway, May 21, 2015, http://www.indianapolismotorspeedway .com/news-multimedia/news/2015/05/21/50000-and-bragging-rights-on-line-for -tag-heuer-pit-stop-challenge.
3. "Pit Stop Challenge," *Wikipedia*, accessed September 12, 2018, https:// en.wikipedia.org/wiki/Pit_Stop_Challenge.

CHAPTER 17

1. "Indianapolis 500 Concerts," *Wikipedia*, accessed October 27, 2018, http:// en.wikipedia.org/wiki/Indianapolis_500_traditions#Concerts.

CHAPTER 18

1. "IRL: IMS Details on the 33rd Annual Last Row Party," Motorsport.com, April 22, 2006, https://www.motorsport.com/indycar/news/irl-ims-details-on -the-33rd-annual-last-row-party/182649/; Hannah Hall, "The Last Row Party's Best Insults," *Indianapolis Monthly*, May 22, 2015, https://www.indianapolismonthly .com/maymadness/last-row-party-best-insults/.

CHAPTER 19

1. Ethan Schwartz, "Drivers Receive Final Instructions at Public Drivers' Meeting," Indianapolis Motor Speedway, May 26, 2018, https://www.indianapolismotorspeedway.com/news-multimedia/news/2018/05/26/drivers-receive-final-instructions-at-public-drivers-meeting-2018.
2. "Indianapolis 500 Public Drivers' Meeting," *Wikipedia*, accessed September 12, 2018, http://en.wikipedia.org/wiki/Indianapolis_500_traditions#Public_Drivers_Meeting_.2F_Legends_Day.

CHAPTER 20

1. "Indianapolis 500 Traditions," *Wikipedia*, accessed September 12, 2018, https://en.wikipedia.org/wiki/Indianapolis_500_traditions#Public_drivers'_meeting_and_Legends_Day.

CHAPTER 21

1. "History of 500 Festival: Celebrating the Spirit and Legacy of the Indianapolis 500," About Us, 500 Festival, accessed October 1, 2018, https://www.500festival.com/about-us/history-of-500festival/.
2. "Overview: Cultivating Indiana's Next Generation of Leaders," 500 Festival Princess Program, Accessed September 25, 2018. https://www.500festival.com/college-programs/princess-program/overview/.
3. "History of 500 Festival," 500 Festival.

CHAPTER 22

1. "Indianapolis 500 Coke Lot," *Wikipedia*, accessed September 18, 2018, http://en.wikipedia.org/wiki/Indianapolis_500_traditions#Coke_Lot.

CHAPTER 23

1. "Indianapolis 500 Snake Pit," *Wikipedia*, accessed September 12, 2018, http://en.wikipedia.org/wiki/Indianapolis_500_traditions#The_Snake_Pit.

CHAPTER 24

1. "Armed Forces Day History," Armed Forces Day, US Department of Defense, accessed September 24, 2018, https://afd.defense.gov/History/.
2. Paul X. Rutz, "Defense Department Honors Indy Motor Speedway," *DoD News*, US Department of Defense, March 8, 2006, http://archive.defense.gov/news/newsarticle.aspx?id=15238.
3. Rutz, "Defense Department Honors Indy Motor Speedway."
4. Rutz, "Defense Department Honors Indy Motor Speedway."

CHAPTER 25

1. "Indy 500 Traditions and FAQs," Indianapolis Motor Speedway, accessed September 21, 2018, http://www.indianapolismotorspeedway.com/events /indy500/history/indy-500-traditions-faqs/faqs.

CHAPTER 26

1. Kara Kavensky, "The Gordon Pipers: A Family Tradition," Town Post Network, March 2, 2015, http://www.townepost.com/indiana/broad-ripple /gordon-pipers-family-tradition/.
2. "History," Indianapolis 500 Gordon Pipers, accessed September 20, 2018, www.500gordonpipers.com/history.html.

PART 3

1. "The 100th Running of The Indianapolis 500 Mile Race Program," Indianapolis Motor Speedway, May 2016.

CHAPTER 28

1. Tom Surber, "Indianapolis 500 Parade of Bands Recognized by Indianapolis House/Senate Resolution," News & Multimedia, Indianapolis Motor Speedway, January 26, 2015, www.indianapolismotorspeedway.com/news-multimedia /news/2015/01/26/indianapolis-500-parade-of-bands-90-anniversary?startrow=4.
2. Surber, "Indianapolis 500 Parade of Bands Recognized by Indianapolis House/Senate Resolution."

CHAPTER 29

1. "Overview: Cultivating Indiana's Next Generation of Leaders," 500 Festival Princess Program, accessed September 25, 2018, https://www.500festival.com /college-programs/princess-program/overview/.

CHAPTER 30

1. "Purdue All-American Marching Band," Wikipedia, accessed September 30, 2018, http://en.wikipedia.org/wiki/Purdue_All-American_Marching_Band.
2. Kelsey Schnieders Lefever, "Counting Toward a Century, Purdue 'All-American' Marching Band Part of Indy 500 Festivities," May 24, 2018, https://www.purdue.edu/newsroom/releases/2018/Q2/counting -toward-a-century,-purdue-all-american-marching-band-part-of-indy -500-festivities.html.

3. "Purdue Big Bass Drum," *Wikipedia*, accessed September 30, 2018, https://en.wikipedia.org/wiki/Purdue_Big_Bass_Drum.

4. "The Golden Girl: History," Purdue Bands & Orchestras, Purdue University, accessed September 30, 2018, https://www.purdue.edu/bands/ensembles/auxiliaries/the-golden-girl/history/.

CHAPTER 31

1. "Indianapolis 500 Traditions," *Wikipedia*, accessed September 21, 2018, http://en.wikipedia.org/wiki/Indianapolis_500_traditions#Celebrity_guests.

CHAPTER 32

1. Paul Dresser, "On the Banks of the Wabash, Far Away," Sheet music (New York: Howley, Haviland & Co, 1897).

CHAPTER 33

1. "Indianapolis 500 Other Songs," *Wikipedia*, accessed September 9, 2018, https://en.wikipedia.org/wiki/Indianapolis_500_traditions#Other_songs.

CHAPTER 34

1. "Indianapolis 500 National Anthem," *Wikipedia*, accessed September 28, 2018. http://en.wikipedia.org/wiki/Indianapolis_500_traditions#National_anthem.

CHAPTER 35

1. "Indianapolis 500 Traditions," *Wikipedia*, accessed September 10, 2018, http://en.wikipedia.org/wiki/Indianapolis_500_traditions#Pre_race_ceremonies; "Indy 500 Flyovers Bring 'Fast Forward' Theme Full-Circle in Patriotic Fashion," News & Multimedia, Indianapolis Motor Speedway, accessed September 10, 2018, https://www.indianapolismotorspeedway.com/events/indy500/news-multimedia/news/2016/05/04/indy-500-flyovers-bring-fast-forward-theme-full-circle-2016; Mathew McClellan, "B-2 Flyover Captivates Hoosiers," RTV6 [ABC], Scripps Media, Inc., May 27, 2018, https://www.theindychannel.com/news/local-news/hamilton-county/b-2-flyover-captivates-hoosiers.

CHAPTER 36

1. "IRL: Indy 500—Billy Graham to Give Race Day Invocation," Motorsport.com, accessed September 22, 2018, https://www.motorsport.com/indycar/news/irl-indy-500-billy-graham-to-give-race-day-invocation/.

2. "The 500 Is More Than Just a Race," *Lakeland Ledger*, May 29, 1977, 7D, accessed September 22, 2018, https://news.google.com/newspapers?id

=ZHVhAAAAIBAJ&sjid=-voDAAAAIBAJ&pg=4159,7848240&dq=jim%20
mckay%201975%20indianapolis&hl=en.

3. "Indianapolis 500 Invocation," *Wikipedia*, accessed October 6, 2018, https://
en.wikipedia.org/wiki/Indianapolis_500_traditions#Invocation.

CHAPTER 37

1. "Indianapolis 500 Taps," *Wikipedia*, accessed September 22, 2018, http://
en.wikipedia.org/wiki/Indianapolis_500_traditions#Taps.

CHAPTER 38

1. "Indianapolis 500 Taps," *Wikipedia*, accessed September 22, 2018, http://
en.wikipedia.org/wiki/Indianapolis_500_traditions#Taps.

CHAPTER 39

1. "Indy 500 Traditions and FAQs," Indianapolis Motor Speedway, accessed
September 21, 2018, https://www.indianapolismotorspeedway.com/events
/indy500/history/indy-500-traditions-faqs/traditions.

2. James F. Hanley and Ballard MacDonald, "Back Home Again in Indiana"
(New York: Paull-Pioneer Music Corp., 1917).

CHAPTER 41

1. Donald Davidson, *The Talk of Gasoline Alley with Donald Davidson*, 1070the-
fan, accessed September 12, 2018, http://www.1070thefan.com/.

2. Davidson, *The Talk of Gasoline Alley with Donald Davidson*.

3. Floyd Clymer, *500 Yearbooks*, 1946–67.

4. Donald Davidson, *The Talk of Gasoline Alley with Donald Davidson*.

5. Floyd Clymer, *500 Yearbooks*, 1946–67.

6. Floyd Clymer, *500 Yearbooks*, 1946–67.

7. Donald Davidson, "The Command: Sid Collins' 30 Days in May," *The Talk of
Gasoline Alley*, 1070thefan, accessed September 12, 2018, http://www.1070thefan.com/.

8. Wilber Shaw, *Gentlemen, Start Your Engines*, ed. Albert W. Bloemker
(New York: Coward-McCann, 1955).

9. ABC-TV, *1977 Indianapolis 500* [telecast], May 29, 1977.

10. ABC-TV, *1977 Indianapolis 500*.

11. ABC-TV, *1977 Indianapolis 500*.

CHAPTER 42

1. Donald Davidson and Rick Shaffer, *Autocourse Official History of The Indianapolis 500*, 2nd ed. (Worcestershire, UK: Icon Publishing Limited, 2013).

2. Davidson and Shaffer, *Autocourse Official History of The Indianapolis 500,* 2nd ed.

3. "Indianapolis 500 Pace Cars," *Wikipedia,* accessed October 28, 2018, http://en.wikipedia.org/wiki/Indianapolis_500_pace_cars.

CHAPTER 43

1. "Riley Hospital Trauma Survivor and Coach Pagano to Make Big Indy 500 Entrance," IU Health (blog). May 23, 2013, https://archive.li/oxiho.

2. "Indianapolis 500 Honorary Starter," *Wikipedia,* accessed October 6, 2018, http://en.wikipedia.org/wiki/Indianapolis_500_traditions#Honorary_starter.

CHAPTER 45

1. "Indy 500 Traditions and FAQs," Indianapolis Motor Speedway, accessed September 21, 2018, http://www.indianapolismotorspeedway.com/events/indy500/history/indy-500-traditions-faqs/faqs; Donald Davidson, Indianapolis Motor Speedway track historian, personal communication, 2016.

CHAPTER 46

1. "Yard of Bricks & Pagoda," Indianapolis Motor Speedway, accessed September 12, 2018, http://www.indianapolismotorspeedway.com/at-the-track/yard-of-bricks-pagoda/the-pagoda.

2. Leslie Bailey, "The Stories Behind Your Favorite Indianapolis 500 Traditions," *IndyStar,* May 1, 2014, https://www.indystar.com/story/entertainment/2014/05/01/indy-500-traditions/8561391/; Janice Unger, "Start Your Engines! Traditions of the Indianapolis 500," The Henry Ford (blog), accessed September 29, 2018, https://www.thehenryford.org/explore/blog/start-your-engines!-traditions-of-the-indianapolis-500.

CHAPTER 47

1. Curt Cavin, "66 Days to the 100th Indy 500: History of the Borg-Warner Trophy," *USA Today,* March 24, 2016, http://sports.usatoday.com/2016/03/24/66-days-to-the-100th-indy-500-history-of-the-borgwarner-trophy/.

2. "Borg-Warner Trophy," Indianapolis Motor Speedway, accessed October 1, 2018, https://www.indianapolismotorspeedway.com/events/indy500/history/borg-warner-trophy.

3. BorgWarner, Inc., "The Borg-Warner Trophy," BorgWarner.com, accessed September 28, 2018, https://www.borgwarner.com/newsroom/the-indianapolis-500.

CHAPTER 48

1. Eric Smith, "Top 10 Thursday: Top 10 Indy 500 Traditions," BleacherReport
.com, May 12, 2011, https://bleacherreport.com/articles/695563-top-ten
-thursday-top-10-indy-500-traditions.

2. Ryan O'Gara, "Florist Has Perfected Indy 500 Wreath for Decades,"
The Herald, May 31, 2016, https://duboiscountyherald.com/b/yorktown-florist
-has-perfected-indy-500-wreath-for-decades.

3. Joe Ruley, "The Woman Behind the Indy 500 Winner's Wreath," *Indianapolis Monthly*, May 24, 2014, https://www.indianapolismonthly.com/maymadness
/the-woman-behind-the-indy-500-winners-wreath/.

CHAPTER 49

1. "Women of the Indianapolis 500," Indianapolis Motor Speedway, accessed
October 1, 2018, https://www.indianapolismotorspeedway.com/events/indy500
/history/women-drivers.

CHAPTER 50

1. Jeanine Head Miller, "Fast Cars and Warm Quilts: Auto Racing's 'Quilt
Lady,'" The Henry Ford, May 2010, accessed October 1, 2018, http://ophelia.sdsu
.edu:8080/henryford_org/12-08-2013/exhibits/pic/2010/10_may.asp.html#more.

2. Armen Hareyan, "Skilled Handiwork of 'Quilt Lady' Has Become Indy
500 Tradition," Huliq.com, May 27, 2007, http://www.huliq.com/22805
/skilled-handiwork-of-quilt-lady-has-become-indy-500-tradition.

3. David M. Brown, "Jeanetta Holder: 'The Quilt Lady,'" Highline Autos,
November 2016, accessed October 1, 2018, https://www.highline-autos.com
/jeanetta-holder-the-quilt-lady/.

CHAPTER 52

1. Dan McGowan, "IMS Shifts Winners Ring Supplier," Inside Indiana
Business, May 12, 2017, http://www.insideindianabusiness.com/story/35417541
/ims-shifts-winners-ring-supplier.

2. "Jostens Joins IMS Family, Will Supply Indianapolis 500 Winner's
Ring," Indianapolis Motor Speedway, May 12, 2017, https://www
.indianapolismotorspeedway.com/news-multimedia/news/2017/05/12
/jostens-joins-ims-family-will-supply-indy-500-winners-ring-2017.

CHAPTER 53

1. Indianapolis Motor Speedway Centennial Era, *The Spirit of the Indianapolis
Motor Speedway* [Video], 2009.

APPENDIX

1. "World Population Day: July 11, 2018," US Census Bureau, July 11, 2018, https://www.census.gov/newsroom/stories/2018/world-population.html.

2. "U.S. Population (Live)," Worldometers.com, accessed October 1, 2018, www.worldometers.info/world-population/us-population/.

3. "Indianapolis, Indiana Population 6-3-2018," World Population Review, accessed October 1, 2018, http://worldpopulationreview.com/us-cities /indianapolis-population/.

4. "Indianapolis, Indiana Population 6-3-2018," World Population Review.

5. "CPI Inflation Calculator," Official Data Foundation, accessed October 1, 2018, http://www.in2013dollars.com/1909-dollars-in-2018?amount=1.

6. "The World When IMS Opened," Indianapolis Motor Speedway, accessed October 1, 2018, https://www.indianapolismotorspeedway.com/history /the-world-when-ims-opened.

7. "Centennial Era," Indianapolis Motor Speedway, accessed October 1, 2018, https://www.indianapolismotorspeedway.com/history/centennial-era.

8. "Centennial Era," Indianapolis Motor Speedway.

Bibliography

ABC-TV. *1977 Indianapolis 500* [telecast]. May 29, 1977.

Associated Press. "Carnegie Retiring after 61 Years as Voice of the Speedway." *USA Today*, June 14, 2006. https://usatoday30.usatoday.com/sports/motor/irl/2006-06-14-carnegie-retirement_x.htm.

Bailey, Leslie. "The Stories Behind Your Favorite Indianapolis 500 Traditions." *IndyStar*, May 1, 2014. https://www.indystar.com/story/entertainment/2014/05/01/indy-500-traditions/8561391/.

Bell, Amanda. "Mom Unser's Chili: A Hot Indy 500 Tradition." *IndyStar*, May 1, 2014. https://www.indystar.com/story/life/food/2014/05/01/mom-unsers-chili-hot-indy-tradition/8577767/.

BorgWarner, Inc. "The Borg-Warner Trophy." BorgWarner.com. Accessed September 28, 2018. https://www.borgwarner.com/newsroom/the-indianapolis-500.

Brown, David M. "Jeanetta Holder: 'The Quilt Lady.'" Highline Autos, November 2016. Accessed October 1, 2018. https://www.highline-autos.com/jeanetta-holder-the-quilt-lady/.

Cavin, Curt. "66 Days to the 100th Indy 500: History of the Borg-Warner Trophy." *USA Today*, March 24, 2016. http://sports.usatoday.com/2016/03/24/66-days-to-the-100th-indy-500-history-of-the-borgwarner-trophy/.

Davidson, Donald. "The Command: Sid Collins' 30 Days in May." *The Talk of Gasoline Alley*. 1070thefan. Accessed September 12, 2018. http://www.1070thefan.com/.

Davidson, Donald. *Indianapolis Motor Speedway: A History*. Indianapolis, IN: Indianapolis Motor Speedway Museum, 1956.

Davidson, Donald. *Indianapolis Motor Speedway Hall of Fame*. Grounds tour audio.

Davidson, Donald. *Indianapolis Motor Speedway Hall of Fame*. Museum video.

Davidson, Donald. *The Talk of Gasoline Alley with Donald Davidson*. 1070thefan. Accessed September 12, 2018. http://www.1070thefan.com/.

Davidson, Donald, and Rick Shaffer. "The Early Years." In *Autocourse Official History of the Indianapolis 500*, 2nd ed., 1–103. Worcestershire, UK: Icon Publishing Limited, 2012.

Davidson, Donald, and Rick Shaffer. *Autocourse Official History of the Indianapolis 500*, 2nd ed. Worcestershire, UK: Icon Publishing Limited, 2012.

Dresser, Paul. "On the Banks of the Wabash, Far Away." Sheet music. New York: Howley, Haviland & Co, 1897.

500 Festival. "History of 500 Festival: Celebrating the Spirit and Legacy of the Indianapolis 500." About Us. Accessed October 1, 2018, https://www.500festival.com/about-us/history-of-500festival/.

500 Festival. "Overview: Cultivating Indiana's Next Generation of Leaders." 500 Festival Princess Program. Accessed September 25, 2018. https://www.500festival.com/college-programs/princess-program/overview/.

"The 500 Is More Than Just a Race." *Lakeland Ledger*, May 29, 1977, 7D. Accessed September 22, 2018. https://news.google.com/newspapers?id=ZHVhAAA AIBAJ&sjid=-voDAAAAIBAJ&pg=4159,7848240&dq=jim%20mckay%20 1975%20indianapolis&hl=en.

Habel, Steve. "Indy's Brickyard Crossing Has Unique Setting and Plenty to Like." *Golf Daily*, May 14, 2018. http://www.golfdaily.com/indys -brickyard-crossing-has-unique-setting-and-plenty-to-like/.

Hall, Hannah. "The Last Row Party's Best Insults." *Indianapolis Monthly*, May 22, 2015. https://www.indianapolismonthly.com/maymadness /last-row-party-best-insults/.

Hanley, James F., and Ballard MacDonald. "Back Home Again in Indiana." New York: Paull-Pioneer Music Corp., 1917.

Hareyan, Armen. "Skilled Handiwork of 'Quilt Lady' Has Become Indy 500 Tradition." Huliq.com, May 27, 2007. http://www.huliq.com/22805 /skilled-handiwork-of-quilt-lady-has-become-indy-500-tradition.

Hickman, Brett. "'Mr. First in Line' of the Indy 500." *The Southsider Voice*, January 1, 2016. http://www.southsidervoice.com/car-nutz/mr-first-in-line-of-the-indy-500.

Indianapolis 500 Gordon Pipers. "History." Accessed September 20, 2018, www.500gordonpipers.com/history.html.

Indianapolis Motor Speedway. "Borg-Warner Trophy." Accessed October 1, 2018. https://www.indianapolismotorspeedway.com/events/indy500/history /borg-warner-trophy.

Indianapolis Motor Speedway. "Centennial Era." Accessed October 1, 2018. https://www.indianapolismotorspeedway.com/history/centennial-era.

Indianapolis Motor Speedway. "$50,000 and Bragging Rights on Line at TAG Heuer Pit Stop Challenge." May 21, 2015. http://www.indianapolismotorspeedway.com /news-multimedia/news/2015/05/21/50000-and-bragging-rights-on-line-for-tag -heuer-pit-stop-challenge.

Indianapolis Motor Speedway. "Indianapolis 500 Historical Stats." Accessed October 6, 2018. http://www.indianapolismotorspeedway

.com/events/indy500/history/historical-stats/race-stats/records/track
-records-qualifications.

Indianapolis Motor Speedway. "Indianapolis Motor Speedway Broken Speed
Barriers—Qualifications." Accessed October 6, 2018. https://www.indiana
polismotorspeedway.com/events/indy500/history/historical-stats/race-stats
/records/broken-speed-barriers.

Indianapolis Motor Speedway. "Indianapolis Motor Speedway Indianapolis 500 Race
Records." Accessed October 6, 2018. http://www.indianapolismotorspeedway
.com/events/indy500/history/historical-stats/race-stats/summaries/track
-records-race.

Indianapolis Motor Speedway. "Indianapolis Motor Speedway Indianapolis 500
Winners." Accessed October 6, 2018. http://www.indianapolismotorspeedway
.com/events/indy500/history/historical-stats/race-stats/summaries
/indianapolis-500-race-winners.

Indianapolis Motor Speedway. "Indy 500 Flyovers Bring 'Fast Forward' Theme Full-
Circle in Patriotic Fashion." News & Multimedia. Accessed September 10, 2018.
https://www.indianapolismotorspeedway.com/events/indy500/news-multimedia
/news/2016/05/04/indy-500-flyovers-bring-fast-forward-theme-full-circle-2016.

Indianapolis Motor Speedway. "Indy 500 Traditions and FAQs." Accessed
September 21, 2018. http://www.indianapolismotorspeedway.com/events
/indy500/history/indy-500-traditions-faqs/traditions.

Indianapolis Motor Speedway. "Jostens Joins IMS Family, Will Supply
Indianapolis 500 Winner's Ring." May 12, 2017. https://www
.indianapolismotorspeedway.com/news-multimedia/news/2017/05/12
/jostens-joins-ims-family-will-supply-indy-500-winners-ring-2017.

Indianapolis Motor Speedway. "The Tom Carnegie Legacy." Accessed June 18,
2018. http://www.indianapolismotorspeedway.com/events/indy500/history
/tom-carnegie-legacy.

Indianapolis Motor Speedway. "Women of the Indianapolis 500." Accessed
October 1, 2018. https://www.indianapolismotorspeedway.com/events
/indy500/history/women-drivers.

Indianapolis Motor Speedway. "The World When IMS Opened." Accessed
October 1, 2018. http://www.indianapolismotorspeedway.com/history
/the-world-when-ims-opened.

Indianapolis Motor Speedway. "Yard of Bricks & Pagoda." Accessed September
12, 2018. http://www.indianapolismotorspeedway.com/at-the-track
/yard-of-bricks-pagoda/yard-of-bricks.

Indianapolis Motor Speedway Centennial Era. *The Spirit of the Indianapolis Motor
Speedway* [Video]. 2009. Accessed September 12, 2018. https://www.youtube
.com/watch?v=orN97dsoUjY.

Indianapolis Motor Speedway Museum. "Plan Your Visit." Accessed September 12, 2018. indyracingmuseum.org/plan-your-visit.

IndySpeedway.com. "Indy 500 Pace Cars." Accessed September 20, 2018. http://indymotorspeedway.com/v1/500pace.htm.

IndySpeedway.com. "Older Indy 500 Qualifying History." Accessed September 12, 2018. http://indymotorspeedway.com/qualifying.html#indy500.

IU Health. "Riley Hospital Trauma Survivor and Coach Pagano to Make Big Indy 500 Entrance." IU Health (blog). May 23, 2013. https://archive.li/0xiho.

Kavensky, Kara. "The Gordon Pipers: A Family Tradition." Town Post Network, March 2, 2015. http://www.townepost.com/indiana/broad-ripple/gordon -pipers-family-tradition/.

Kennedy, Pat. *Indy 500 Recaps: The Short Chute Edition.* Bloomington, IN: AuthorRHouse, 2012.

Lefever, Kelsey Schnieders. "Counting Toward a Century, Purdue 'All-American' Marching Band Part of Indy 500 Festivities." May 24, 2018. https://www .purdue.edu/newsroom/releases/2018/Q2/counting-toward-a-century, -purdue-all-american-marching-band-part-of-indy-500-festivities.html.

McClellan, Mathew. "B-2 Flyover Captivates Hoosiers." RTV6 [ABC], Scripps Media, Inc., May 27, 2018. https://www.theindychannel.com/news /local-news/hamilton-county/b-2-flyover-captivates-hoosiers.

McGowan, Dan. "IMS Shifts Winners Ring Supplier." Inside Indiana Business, May 12, 2017. http://www.insideindianabusiness.com/story/35417541 /ims-shifts-winners-ring-supplier.

Miller, Jeanine Head. "Fast Cars and Warm Quilts: Auto Racing's 'Quilt Lady.'" The Henry Ford, May 2010. Accessed October 1, 2018. http://ophelia .sdsu.edu:8080/henryford_org/12-08-2013/exhibits/pic/2010/10_may.asp .html#more.

Mitchell, Dawn. "Why It's Called Carb Day When Indy Cars Don't Use Carburetors." IndyStar.com, May 25, 2018. https://www.indystar.com/story /sports/motor/indy-500/2018/05/25/indy-500-tradition-carb-day-without -carburetors-indycar/611285002./

Motorsport.com. "IRL: IMS Details on the 33rd Annual Last Row Party." April 22, 2006. https://www.motorsport.com/indycar/news/irl-ims-details -on-the-33rd-annual-last-row-party/182649/.

Motorsport.com. "IRL: IMS Presents Indianapolis 500 Traditions." May 3, 2006. https://www.motorsport.com/us/indycar/news/irl-ims-presents-indianapolis -500-traditions/2082202/.

Motorsport.com. "IRL: Indy 500—Billy Graham to Give Race Day Invocation." Accessed September 22, 2018. https://www.motorsport.com/indycar/news /irl-indy-500-billy-graham-to-give-race-day-invocation/.

O'Gara, Ryan. "Florist Has Perfected Indy 500 Wreath for Decades." *The Herald*, May 31, 2016. https://duboiscountyherald.com/b/yorktown-florist-has -perfected-indy-500-wreath-for-decades.

Official Data Foundation. "CPI Inflation Calculator." Accessed October 1, 2018. http://www.in2013dollars.com/1909-dollars-in-2018?amount=1.

Phillips, George. "The Origins of the IMS Yellow Shirt." *Oil Pressure* (blog), May 7, 2013. https://oilpressure.wordpress.com/2013/05/07/the-origins-of-the-ims -yellow-shirt/.

Price, Nelson. "He's On It." *Traces of Indiana and Midwestern History*. Indianapolis: Indiana Historical Society, 2015, 27 (1): 14–21.

Purdue University. "The Golden Girl: History." Purdue Bands & Orchestras. Accessed September 30, 2018. https://www.purdue.edu/bands/ensembles /auxiliaries/the-golden-girl/history/.

Riffle, Jeremy, and Suzi Elliott. *Fact Sheet*. Indianapolis, IN: The Indianapolis Motor Speedway Media Center, 2014.

Ruley, Joe. "The Woman Behind the Indy 500 Winner's Wreath." *Indianapolis Monthly*, May 24, 2014. https://www.indianapolismonthly.com/maymadness /the-woman-behind-the-indy-500-winners-wreath/.

Rutz, Paul X. "Defense Department Honors Indy Motor Speedway." *DoD News*, US Department of Defense, March 8, 2006. http://archive.defense.gov/news /newsarticle.aspx?id=15238.

Schmitz, Brian. "Gates May Be Closing on Indy 500 Tradition." *Orlando Sentinel*, May 12, 1987. http://articles.orlandosentinel.com/1987-05-12/sports /0130070041_1_bisceglia-first-in-line-indy.

Schwartz, Ethan. "Drivers Receive Final Instructions at Public Drivers' Meeting." Indianapolis Motor Speedway, May 26, 2018. https://www .indianapolismotorspeedway.com/news-multimedia/news/2018/05/26 /drivers-receive-final-instructions-at-public-drivers-meeting-2018.

Shaw, Wilber. *Gentlemen, Start Your Engines*. Edited by Albert W. Bloemker. New York: Coward-McCann, 1955.

Shaw, Wilbur, and Al Bloemker. *500 Miles to Go*. New York, NY: Coward-McCann, 1961.

Smith, Eric. "Top 10 Thursday: Top 10 Indy 500 Traditions." BleacherReport.com, May 12, 2011. https://bleacherreport.com/articles/695563-top-ten-thursday -top-10-indy-500-traditions.

Surber, Tom. "Indianapolis 500 Parade of Bands Recognized by Indianapolis House/Senate Resolution." News & Multimedia, Indianapolis Motor Speedway. January 26, 2015. www.indianapolismotorspeedway.com /news-multimedia/news/2015/01/26/indianapolis-500-parade-of -bands-90-anniversary?startrow=4.

Unger, Janice. "Start Your Engines! Traditions of the Indianapolis 500." The Henry Ford (blog). Accessed September 29, 2018. https://www.thehenryford.org/explore/blog/start-your-engines!-traditions-of-the-indianapolis-500/.

US Census Bureau. "World Population Day: July 11, 2018." July 11, 2018. https://www.census.gov/newsroom/stories/2018/world-population.html.

US Department of Defense. "Armed Forces Day History." Armed Forces Day. Accessed September 24, 2018. https://afd.defense.gov/History/.

Weintraut, Linda, and Jane Nolan. "In the Public Interest." In *Oral Histories of Hoosier Broadcaster*, 110–120. Indianapolis: Indiana Historical Society, 1999.

Wikipedia contributors. "Indianapolis 500 Celebrity Guests." *Wikipedia, The Free Encyclopedia*. Accessed September 21, 2018. http://en.wikipedia.org/wiki/Indianapolis_500_traditions#Celebrity_guests.

Wikipedia contributors. "Indianapolis 500 Coke Lot." *Wikipedia, The Free Encyclopedia*. Accessed September 18, 2018. http://en.wikipedia.org/wiki/Indianapolis_500_traditions#Coke_Lot.

Wikipedia contributors. "Indianapolis 500 Concerts." *Wikipedia, The Free Encyclopedia*. Accessed October 27, 2018. http://en.wikipedia.org/wiki/Indianapolis_500_traditions#Concerts.

Wikipedia contributors. "Indianapolis 500 Honorary Starter." *Wikipedia, The Free Encyclopedia*. Accessed October 6, 2018. http://en.wikipedia.org/wiki/Indianapolis_500_traditions#Honorary_starter.

Wikipedia contributors. "Indianapolis 500 Invocation." *Wikipedia, The Free Encyclopedia*. Accessed October 6, 2018. http://en.wikipedia.org/wiki/Indianapolis_500_traditions#Invocation.

Wikipedia contributors. "Indianapolis 500 National Anthem." *Wikipedia, The Free Encyclopedia*. Accessed September 28, 2018. http://en.wikipedia.org/wiki/Indianapolis_500_traditions#National_anthem.

Wikipedia contributors. "Indianapolis 500 Other Songs." *Wikipedia, The Free Encyclopedia*. Accessed September 9, 2018. http://en.wikipedia.org/wiki/Indianapolis_500_traditions#Other_songs.

Wikipedia contributors. "Indianapolis 500 Pace Cars." *Wikipedia, The Free Encyclopedia*. Accessed October 28, 2018. http://en.wikipedia.org/wiki/Indianapolis_500_pace_cars.

Wikipedia contributors. "Indianapolis 500 Public Drivers' Meeting." *Wikipedia, The Free Encyclopedia*. Accessed September 12, 2018. http://en.wikipedia.org/wiki/Indianapolis_500_traditions#Public_Drivers_Meeting_.2F_Legends_Day.

Wikipedia contributors. "Indianapolis 500 Snake Pit." *Wikipedia, The Free Encyclopedia*. Accessed September 12, 2018. http://en.wikipedia.org/wiki/Indianapolis_500_traditions#The_Snake_Pit.

Wikipedia contributors. "Indianapolis 500 Taps." *Wikipedia, The Free Encyclo-pedia*. Accessed September 22, 2018. http://en.wikipedia.org/wiki/Indianapolis_500_traditions#Taps.

Wikipedia contributors. "Indianapolis 500 Traditions." *Wikipedia, The Free Encyclopedia*. Accessed October 27, 2018. http://en.wikipedia.org/wiki/Indianapolis_500_traditions.

Wikipedia contributors. "Pit Stop Challenge." *Wikipedia, The Free Encyclopedia*. Accessed September 12, 2018. https://en.wikipedia.org/wiki/Pit_Stop_Challenge.

Wikipedia contributors. "Purdue All-American Marching Band." *Wikipedia, The Free Encyclopedia*. Accessed September 30, 2018. http://en.wikipedia.org/wiki/Purdue_All-American_Marching_Band.

Wikipedia contributors. "Purdue Big Bass Drum." *Wikipedia, The Free Encyclo-pedia*. Accessed September 30, 2018. https://en.wikipedia.org/wiki/Purdue_Big_Bass_Drum.

Worldometers.com. "U.S. Population (Live)." Accessed October 1, 2018. www.worldometers.info/world-population/us-population/.

World Population Review. "Indianapolis, Indiana Population 6-3-2018." Accessed October 1, 2018. http://worldpopulationreview.com/us-cities/indianapolis-population/.

Index

Page numbers in *italics* indicate photographs.

JAMES CRAIG REINHARDT is an official tour guide for the Indianapolis Motor Speedway Museum and the author of *The Winning Cars of the Indianapolis 500.*